Stupid
PC Tricks

Stupid
PC Tricks

Bob LeVitus
with
Ed Tittel

Addison-Wesley Publishing Company, Inc.

Reading, Massachusetts ◊ Menlo Park, California ◊ New York ◊
Don Mills, Ontario ◊ Wokingham, England ◊ Amsterdam ◊ Bonn ◊
Sydney ◊ Singapore ◊ Tokyo ◊ Madrid ◊ San Juan ◊ Paris ◊ Seoul ◊
Milan ◊ Mexico City ◊ Taipei

Many of the designations used by manufacturers and sellers to distinguish their products are claimed as trademarks. Where those designations appear in this book and Addison-Wesley was aware of a trademark claim, the designations have been printed in initial capital letters (e.g., Spirograph).

Library of Congress Cataloging-in-Publication Data

LeVitus, Bob.
    Stupid PC tricks / Bob LeVitus with Ed Tittel.
        p.   cm.
    ISBN 0-201-57759-3
    1. IBM Personal Computer--Programming. I. Tittel, Ed.
  II. Title.
QA76.8.I1015L48   1991
005.265--dc20   91-1993
                                         CIP

Associate Editor: Rachel Guichard
Technical Reviewers: Enrique LaRoche and Rose Malle-Gianattassio
Cover design by Ronn Campisi
Text design by Joyce Weston
Set in 11-point Bitstream *Latin 725* by Bob LeVitus
2 3 4 5 6 7 8 9 10 - MW - 94939291
Second printing, April 1991
ISBN 0-201-57759-3

This book is dedicated to two very important groups: first and foremost, to the intrepid programmers whose work made this book possible, and second, to my family—Suzy, Austin, Chelsea, and Dusty—without whose support and bemused tolerance I never could have finished working on this book.
E. T.

I'll drink to that! To the programmers: we couldn't have done it without you. And to my family—Lisa, Allison, Max, Killer, and Sadie—thanks for putting up with the late nights and weird noises. Last but not least, thanks to my Mom and Dad—I wouldn't be here today if not for them.
B. L.

Acknowledgments

I'd like to thank Jamie Sanders, chief CompuServe Sys*Op for Novell, Inc., who got me interested (and completely hooked) on the whims and wonders of on-line communication. Even more, I'd like to thank Bob LeVitus for inviting me to work on this project with him and for getting me involved in the blissful world of *Stupid PC Tricks*.

E. T.

I'd like to thank the nice folks at CompuServe—too numerous to mention—you know who you are! I'd also like to thank the wonderful folks at Addison-Wesley: Carole McClendon, Joanne Clapp Fullagar, Rachel Guichard, Beth Burleigh, and Abby Genuth. My most heartfelt thanks go to Ed Tittel, whose remarkable contributions make this book what it is. Thanks, Ed. You're awesome, dude.

B. L.

Table of Contents

Introduction

System Requirements

To run Stupid PC Tricks, you need an IBM or IBM-compatible personal computer. By model name, this means a PC, PC/XT, PC/AT, PS/2, or equivalent clone machine with a minimum of 512 KB of random access memory (RAM). From here on out, we'll refer to all these machines generically as a PC. To use the disks supplied with the book, you'll also need a 5.25" floppy drive (if you need 3.5" disks instead, or want uncompressed versions, please send in the order form at the back of the book). Most of the programs should run with any version of DOS numbered 2.0 or higher, but we recommend that you run DOS 3.31 or higher, because that is what all the software was specifically tested with.

We've constructed the disks so that the programs can be run only on a PC with a hard drive, but people who order the decompressed floppies will also get a step-by-step description of how to build a set of disks for a floppy-only machine (this does require access to a PC with a hard drive to set them up for use). In the same vein, most of the tricks will work on a monochrome Hercules, CGA, or EGA monitor, but for the most fun, we recommend a color VGA.

The Test Environment

Our test machines included four different kinds of PCs, which we used to download and try out the original tricks. We then tested the STUP-PC1.EXE and STUP-PC2.EXE files and the tools included along with them to make sure that all the tricks worked (and to find out which ones required color monitors).

We then distributed the "golden" release file of our tricks to a few interested parties for further review. Throughout the process, we made sure that everything worked as expected.

We can't guarantee that our tricks will work on your PC, nor can we safeguard you from harm. Hopefully, the array of machines, CPU types, and operating system versions tested will prove encouraging. Chances are that most, if not all, of the tricks will work for you, as long as you follow the installation instructions.

Here's what we used to test the Stupid PC Tricks (SPCTs):

Machine 1: A hybrid 386SX

- 16 MHz 80386SX Magitronics motherboard; AMI BIOS
- 5 MB RAM
- 43 MB Micropolis hard disk, WD 1003 controller
- MS-DOS 3.31
- Samsung CJ4681 VGA display, CompuAdd 16-bit VGA card

Machine 2: Compaq Portable 386/20

- 20 MHz 80386DX, Compaq BIOS
- 3 MB RAM
- 100 MB Connor IDE hard disk, integrated IDE controller
- Compaq PC-DOS 3.31
- Gas-plasma CGA display

14

Machine 3: Compaq Portable II

- 8 MHz 80286, Compaq BIOS
- 640 KB RAM
- 20 MB MFM hard disk, Compaq integrated controller
- Compaq PC-DOS 2.20, 3.31
- Monochrome EGA display

Machine 4: NEC Portable 386SX Lunchbox

- 16 MHz 80386SX, NEC/Phoenix BIOS
- 2 MB RAM
- 40 MB RLL hard disk, NEC integrated controller
- MS-DOS 3.31
- Monochrome LCD VGA display

How to Install the Tricks

The files on the floppies that come with this book are structured so that you can unpack them to run on a hard disk. As stored on the original 5.25" floppies, these files consume almost the entire capacity of the two 360 kilobyte (KB) disks—together, they total nearly 691 KB, or 706,671 bytes, of information. Since the files are in a compressed format, they will occupy about 1000 KB when restored to their original, uncompressed form.

The first step in the installation process is to copy the files from their original floppies and to uncompress the tricks they contain. If you examine the contents of the disks with the DOS DIR (directory) command, you'll see that each one contains a single file named STUP-PC1.EXE or STUP-PC2.EXE. The second disk also contains an uncompressed file, SMART.BAT, which you will use to set up and guide you through copying and decompressing the tricks files.

Assuming that you want to install the tricks on the C: drive and that you start with the current directory set to C:\, carefully enter the bold text, and you're ready for each trick covered in the following chapters. The explanatory text included in each step describes what is going on.

1. C:\>**COPY A:\SMART.BAT**
   Insert the floppy labeled StupidPC-2 into the A: drive and copy the SMART batch file to your hard disk.

2. C:\>**SMART**
   Runs the SMART program, which prompts you to insert the two Stupid PC Tricks floppies, decompresses the files, and copies the directory creation program, STUPID.BAT, to your root directory (C:\).

3. C:\>**STUPID**
   Runs STUPID.BAT, which sets up a set of subdirectories, one for each trick, and cleans up after itself to make living with the tricks easier for you. Each individual trick is copied into its own subdirectory, after which the original copies are deleted, along with the original, compressed file that started the whole process. This program sets up an easy-to-manage organization for the tricks, and it cleans up after itself to remove duplicate files and the no longer needed compressed files.

4. C:\STUP-PC>**CD **
   Change directory to C:\ (where the files which will be deleted in step 5 are stored).

5. C:\>**DEL STUPID.BAT**
   C:\>**DEL SMART.BAT**
   These two commands complete the post-installation clean-up, removing the batch files that set up the directory structure (STUPID.BAT) and copied the compressed files (SMART.BAT).

Although it's not absolutely necessary to run Step 3, we strongly recommend that you do so, because the rest of the book is written assuming that you have done this prior to installing each trick. If you're a DOS wizard, you can ignore this advice—what's going on is not really all that complicated. If you are not a DOS wizard, please use Step 3 to make things easy on yourself.

When you are looking at a trick for the first time, if the subdirectory in which it lives contains a file named READ.ME or one with the extension .DOC, it's a good idea to read it before proceeding with the installation. We've tried to cover all of the essential points about each trick in its own chapter, but it's always a good idea to consult the original author's tips and information before installing a trick and using it for the first time.

Note: You'll find that we use the term DOS PATH frequently throughout this book. The DOS PATH establishes the way DOS searches for files and is usually included in the AUTOEXEC.BAT file. The DOS PATH tells DOS where to look for things if it can't find them in the current default directory (that is, the directory where you are currently located). It can tell DOS to look in multiple directories on multiple drives and is a very handy way to keep all the programs and commands you regularly use accessible no matter what your current directory may happen to be.

Squeezing the Most out of the SPCT Disk

Now a word about our special compression technology: The tricks are distributed in a .ZIP format, using Phil Katz's PKZIP program to do the compression and his ZIP2EXE program to turn the compressed file into a self-unpacking program. PKZIP and ZIP2EXE are two items in a useful set of compression, decompression, and file management utilities available from PKWARE, Inc. that are widely used in the PC community (they're especially handy for archiving lots of data on a single disk and for compressing files before sending them elsewhere by modem).

We can't recommend these utilities highly enough. If you're interested in obtaining a copy, send $25.00 in U.S. funds to PKWARE, Inc., 7545 North Port Washington Road, Glendale, WI 53217. These utilities can also be found on most on-line information services or bulletin boards, such as CompuServe.

Disclaimer

The authors make no claims about the performance of the tricks on the SPCT disks. We've tested each trick on a variety of PCs, and they all appear to work as advertised in the far from exhaustive testing that we conducted. We feel pretty sure that none of the tricks will do any damage to your PC, such as trashing the hard disk or burning up the motherboard. However, we can make no guarantees—use the tricks at your own risk.

Some tricks may conflict with other programs or TSRs that you normally use. A TSR is a special kind of DOS program, called terminate-and-stay-resident, that is available at any time with a special keystroke. Appendix A, "Managing TSRs," covers TSR basics, and the pros and cons of TSRs, RAM requirements, and tools. Be sure to check Appendix A out; it's worth reading.

Unfortunately, there was no way that we could test every possible combination of DOS programs and TSRs. We sincerely apologize if something doesn't work or doesn't get along well with your current setup, but we cannot be held responsible. All we can say is, "Try them and see!"

We both firmly believe in regular hard disk backups and strongly recommend that you create a fresh backup before installing these disks or trying any of these tricks on yourself or some other, unsuspecting co-worker. If you don't have a backup and things go wrong, you'll have no one to blame but yourself.

Our talented group of beta testers also alerted us to another potential source of trouble: It's particularly important to be careful about using TSRs when running in a networked PC environment. Since most network drivers are themselves TSRs, it's undesirable to add new TSRs (like several of our Stupid PC Tricks) into this kind of environment unless you're an experienced DOS user and can deal with the loss of your networked connection. Because network driver and related TSRs already can consume significant amounts of RAM, adding more overhead to your system will also only diminish the usability of the remaining DOS memory space. We repeat: If you're running on a network, avoid the TSRs in our book unless you're able and willing to troubleshoot possible difficulties that may result.

Warning

These tricks are for entertainment only. We don't recommend using them irresponsibly, whether on a standalone machine or on anybody's network of PCs. If you play tricks on others, stick around to help clean up afterwards—if you don't, you could find yourself in all kinds of trouble. Remember: One person's trick is another person's tribulation.

Avoiding Trouble

Any time you change your DOS environment, especially when you're installing a trick that is a TSR program, it's wise to take a few precautionary steps to avoid conflicts or more serious problems.

To begin with, whenever you change anything, it's a good idea to have a backup of what you started from so you can return to a known working state easily. We recommend that you make regular backups of your entire PC environment in any case. When you're installing or running anything new, start by making a fresh backup. That way, if anything goes awry, you can easily get back to a pristine state.

It's also a good idea to make a bootable floppy that contains your current system directory, along with the two important DOS files that control how your machine behaves when you start it up: CONFIG.SYS, which manages your system configuration, and AUTOEXEC.BAT, which is executed every time you start up your PC. You'll also want to include any other files having the extension .SYS, since these files are typically needed to establish whatever working environment you've built for yourself.

This floppy will prove invaluable if any problems arise. If necessary, you can start your machine using its contents to create a known working environment from which to run your backup software (or from which you can back out changes to your working environment by hand). This floppy can also provide a quick fix for your operating environment and may obviate having to do a complete restore from your backup.

What to Do If Your System Hangs or Crashes

We don't expect that any of the Stupid PC Tricks will cause your system to crash, but in the unlikely event that some interaction between your previous environment and one or more of the tricks causes your machine to hang up or become otherwise inoperable, remember not to panic.

To get yourself going again, first try to reboot your PC by entering the reboot key combination: <Ctrl>-<Alt>-<Del>. If this doesn't work, turn the machine off, wait at least 30 seconds (or until you hear the hard disk quiet down), and then turn it back on. In most cases, the PC will run without further problems. Then you'll have to decide whether you want to figure out what was causing the problem and whether or not you want to use the trick that caused the problem.

If the PC still won't reboot properly, restart it using the backup system floppy and remove the trick that was just installed. Again, you'll have to decide whether or not you want to figure out what's causing the problem or whether it's easier not to use the trick.

If you decide to analyze the situation, here's what you'll have to do: Remove all TSRs (see Appendix A, "Managing TSRs," for more information) and any non-DOS command shells. Install the trick, and then start installing the other components of your working environment one at a time. As you add each one, test your environment for problems. In most cases, when you add the offending program or shell, it will make itself known. This is a time-consuming and painstaking process, but it will enable you to catch the culprit(s) involved.

Contacting the Authors

Feel free to write us care of our publisher, or via CompuServe Electronic Mail: 76376,606.

EXPLOSIV

 "Fireworks for your DOS machine"

What EXPLOSIV Does

EXPLOSIV is a screen blanker that puts firework displays on your screen—in color for color displays and in monochrome for other displays. It can be installed as a TSR (it runs as a normal DOS program by default), making it available as a true screen blanker, one that automatically turns itself on after a predetermined period of keyboard inactivity.

   Of the four screen-blanking utilities included in this book, this one is potentially the most useful. However, its pyrotechnics give it lots of entertainment value, and it also possesses a gentle hypnotic ability that should keep you watching it from time to time, if not regularly.

How to Use EXPLOSIV

To run EXPLOSIV as a program, simply type the program's name at the DOS prompt (e.g., C:\>**STUP-PC\EXPLOSIV\EXPLOSIV**). As long as it's on your DOS PATH, or in your current directory, the fireworks will immediately follow. (For more information on the DOS PATH, see the glossary at the end of the book.) To return to the DOS prompt, strike any key.

21

Using EXPLOSIV as a TSR requires a bit more work than using it as a program, because you can specify a number of options to control the program's behavior (see Figure 1, *EXPLOSIV Options*).

```
EXPLOSIV.COM - Graphics screen saver - version 1.22

        UGA with analog color display detected.

Select arguments from the following :

     ?        display this help screen
     on       deactivate explosiv ( Ctrl-Alt-B )
     off      activate explosiv ( Ctrl-Alt-E )
     new      change characteristics
     mda      for MDA monochrome cards
     cga      for CGA/MCGA graphics cards
     herc     for Hercules graphics cards
     mono     for Mono/color UGA/EGA cards
     vga      for UGA/EGA color cards
     novid    do not use video interrupt
     c<n>     the color ( 1 - 15 )
     d<n>     the delay factor ( 1 - 255 ).
     e<n>     the number of explosions ( 1 - 15 )
     m<n>     become a screen saver, wait n minutes ( 1 - 30 )
     p<n>     number of text pages to save ( 1 - 4 )

Press Ctrl-Alt-Shift to turn screen saver on.

C:\TEST>
```

Figure 1. EXPLOSIV Options:
EXPLOSIV offers numerous hardware and software options.

The following table covers EXPLOSIV's options:

Option	Explanation
d$<n>$	A delay factor to determine the duration and time between explosions (n determines the amount of delay and must be a whole number in the range of 1–255, where 255 is slowest).
e$<n>$	The number of simultaneous explosions to be displayed (n indicates the number of explosions and must be a whole number in the range of 1–15, where 1 displays the most simultaneous explosions).

22

m <*n*>	The number of minutes of inactivity before EXPLOSIV is invoked (*n* indicates the number of minutes and must be a whole number in the range of 1–30, where m30 indicates the maximum, 30-minute inactivity period). Specifying this option in the EXPLOSIV invocation is what causes it to be installed as a TSR.
c<*n*>	The color to use for each explosion (*n* identifies the color by number and must be a whole number in the range 1–15). Since different graphics cards use different numbers to identify colors, only experimentation can show you which numbers map to which colors. This switch also requires use of the mono option (for example, C:\>**EXPLOSIV mono c4** displayed red-only fireworks on our CompuAdd VGA card).
p<*n*>	The number of text pages to save in memory (*n* must be a whole number in the range 1–4). Each text page requires about 4 KB of additional memory for EXPLOSIV and is used to save the existing screen's contents for restoration when EXPLOSIV is stopped and normal operation is restarted (higher numbers are only necessary for large-screen or high-end graphics displays).

Other EXPLOSIV options include those documented in the following table:

Option	Explanation
on	Turns on the first deactivated EXPLOSIV found in memory (EXPLOSIV is written to permit multiple copies of itself to be installed as TSRs and knows how to manage itself).
off	Turns off the first activated EXPLOSIV found in memory.

23

mono	Requests single-color fireworks (with the c<*n*> option).
new	Changes any other options as specified in the current EXPLOSIV invocation for a memory-resident version of EXPLOSIV.
novid	Causes EXPLOSIV to ignore other programs that write to the screen (some DOS programs write information to the screen while executing in the background; this option permits EXPLOSIV to coexist with them without causing incorrect information to be supplied to such programs). Once set, this option cannot be changed (even with the new option).
<mode>	EXPLOSIV detects the type of graphics adapter for the PC's display by default, but <mode> can be used to override the default to operate in one of the following modes: MDA (25x80 character mode only; blanks the screen without any fireworks), CGA (640x200 2-color graphics), herc (720x348 2-color graphics), MONO (640x350 2-color graphics), or VGA (640x350 16-color graphics; displays each explosion in a different color).

Since we did not have access to Hercules graphics adapters in our testing, we can only pass the authors' remarks along that these types of adapters are more likely to have problems with EXPLOSIV than any of the others. If you have a Hercules graphics adapter, make sure you test EXPLOSIV in benign conditions before betting any real work on its correct operation.

Escaping EXPLOSIV

Since EXPLOSIV is a screen blanker, it takes over the screen when executed explicitly or when the keyboard has been idle for a certain period of time. To make EXPLOSIV stop any time it's running, you need only to strike any key on the keyboard; this will automatically restore whatever was displayed when EXPLOSIV took over.

Suggestions for Using EXPLOSIV

We think using EXPLOSIV as a part of your everyday DOS environment is an excellent idea. In fact, we recommend that you include the following line in your AUTOEXEC.BAT file:

C:\STUP-PC\EXPLOSIV\EXPLOSIV E5 M1

This will install EXPLOSIV as a TSR so that it will activate after 60 seconds of idle keyboard time (this is what the M1 parameter tells EXPLOSIV to do) and will include a satisfyingly large number of simultaneous explosions (that is what the E5 switch tells EXPLOSIV to do). The benefits of a screen blanker are hard to realize unless you use one, and we couldn't find a better automatic one than EXPLOSIV.

EXPLOSIV: The Fine Print

EXPLOSIV makes an effective screen blanker, and if you decide to use it as such on a regular basis, not as casual entertainment, you should register your copy by sending a check or money order for $5.00 to Reidar Gresseth, #207 - 2345 West 5th Ave., Vancouver, BC Canada V6K 1S6.

We recommend playing with it; if you like it as much as we do, we hope you'll register and pay the fee. We can do no better than to quote the authors' .MAN file on this subject:

"As this is shareware and not freeware, a payment of 5 dollars is expected if you find EXPLOSIV to be at all useful. This amount should also encourage us to write improved versions of this program."

There's hardly any better value than the registration fees for shareware: It's the only way to get commercial- or near-commercial-quality software at a fraction of the price of a packaged, on-the-shelf program. Helping keep these developers in business is a way of ensuring that software prices stay lower than they would otherwise.

EXPLOSIV: The Files

EXPLOSIV includes two files:

EXPLOSIV.MAN	The documentation for EXPLOSIV (the file extension .MAN is common in the UNIX community, where it indicates a MAN page or manual page, part of a system-wide, on-line documentation system)
EXPLOSIV.COM	The EXPLOSIV program

Kaleidoscope

 "A new view on color PCs"

What Kaleidoscope Does

Kaleidoscope turns your EGA or VGA screen into a pattern display engine whose ever-changing, colorful patterns resemble a kaleidoscope. Because of the program's stunning color capabilities, it is best viewed on a color monitor, but it will work on a monochrome EGA or monochrome VGA display.

How to Use Kaleidoscope

Kaleidoscope is the author's name for his program, but since it is 12 characters long, it is not the name of the actual DOS executable file (.EXE) that makes kaleidoscopic images appear on the screen, nor is it the name of the batch file that starts up the program. To run the program, you have to enter either the name of the batch file, **KALEIDIS.BAT**, or type **C:\STUP-PC\KALEIDIS\KALEIDIS**.

Kaleidoscope offers a number of options to control its execution, as depicted in Figure 2, *Kaleidoscope's Start-up Screen*.

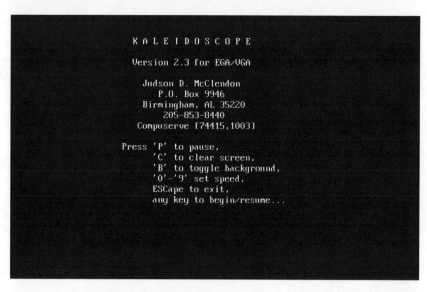

```
          K A L E I D O S C O P E

          Version 2.3 for EGA/VGA

          Judson D. McClendon
              P.O. Box 9946
          Birmingham, AL 35220
              205-853-8440
          Compuserve [74415,1003]

      Press 'P' to pause,
            'C' to clear screen,
            'B' to toggle background,
            '0'-'9' set speed,
            ESCape to exit,
            any key to begin/resume...
```

Figure 2. Kaleidoscope's Start-up Screen:
A simple set of controls for a fascinating display.

The following table explains what the options do.

Key	Key Label/Explanation
P	Pauses and restarts the current Kaleidoscope display.
C	Clears the screen and starts Kaleidoscope again.
B	Changes the background color (default=black).
0–9	Varies the display change rate (0=slow, 9=fast).
<Esc>	Exits Kaleidoscope and returns to DOS.
Any key	Starts Kaleidoscope display.

All that's necessary to run Kaleidoscope is that the program (and the batch file, if you'd prefer) be on the current DOS PATH. (For more information on the DOS PATH, see the glossary at the end of the book.) Entering the filename for either one will cause the startup screen to display, after which you can start the real action at will.

For faster machines, speeding up the display causes a hypnotic succession of swirling images. It's fun to vary the speed and see how it affects what's displayed. Toggling the background can be interesting (each time you toggle the background selection, it switches from black to a solid-color background, or vice versa), but playing with the background is not necessary to enjoy the program's random graphic artistry.

Escaping Kaleidoscope

Pressing <Esc> exits Kaleidoscope and returns you to DOS, but you can also exit Kaleidoscope with other conventional DOS escapes: Both <Ctrl>-C and <Ctrl>-<Break> will work. These alternate methods do, however, litter the screen with status and error messages and, more importantly, they do not reset the EGA or VGA environment to the defaults you've established for your system. We strongly recommend pressing <Esc> as the preferred method to exit Kaleidoscope, primarily because it leaves your graphics display in the state that you'll expect it to be in.

Suggestions for Using Kaleidoscope

Kaleidoscope is a great program to use as a screen blanker, a program whose job it is to keep your computer display busy. If you do not use a screen blanker while you are not using your computer, the phosphors on the display may become damaged and patterns may be etched on the screen from recurring identical displays. By keeping an ever-changing pattern on the screen, screen blankers avoid the potential for such damage.

One disadvantage to Kaleidoscope is that it must be manually started by its user before he or she stops using the machine. Ideally, a screen blanker starts up by itself after a certain period of idle time (see the chapter on EXPLOSIV for an example). Such automatic behavior requires, however, that the program be a TSR (to be able to run at any time, it has to be resident at all times), so Kaleidoscope represents a very nice trade-off between convenience and capabilities.

We can't do justice to Kaleidoscope's infinite variety of varied colors and constant motion in a black-and-white picture. Figure 3, *Kaleidoscope in Black and White,* will give you some idea of what you'll see when you use it. We guarantee that you'll find its activities more entertaining and its displays more fascinating than our monochrome picture. By the way, the higher-resolution color monitors and graphics adapters make Kaleidoscope look better.

Figure 3. Kaleidoscope in Black and White:
A monochrome, static representation of Kaleidoscope's stunning, colorful, moving display.

Kaleidoscope: The Fine Print

Kaleidoscope was programmed by Judson D. McClendon. It is freeware and can be shared with your colleagues and co-workers. Because it has beauty and visual appeal, it's likely to be a big hit both at home and at the office. If you want to send Mr. McClendon any comments or suggestions, you can write to him at 329 37th Court NE, Birmingham, AL 35215.

Kaleidoscope: The Files

The following files are included as a part of Kaleidoscope:

KALEDIS.EXE	Kaleidoscope program
KALEIDIS.BAT	Batch file to execute the KALEDIS program file

BUGLE

 "Heed the trumpet's call!"

What BUGLE Does

BUGLE does what any self-respecting bugler likes to do: It plays bugle calls—*lots* of bugle calls. In fact, both of us bugled a bit in previous avatars in the Boy Scouts of America, and we learned a number of bugle calls from this little gem that we hadn't even heard of before.

How to Use BUGLE

BUGLE is easy to use, just type **C:\STUP-PC\BUGLE\BUGLE**, and you'll be presented with a large menu of bugle calls, all of which the computer will happily play for you (see Figure 4, *Bugle Calls,* to look over the menu).

BUGLE offers 20 bugle calls and is guaranteed to make for a more educated generation of bugle players. Or, for some fun at your desktop, you can instruct BUGLE to play a specific call without giving any indication of what's going on. Bugle's help screen, accessed by typing **99** at the SELECTION? prompt, gives on-line instructions to accomplish this trick (see Figure 5, *Bugle Help*). You simply type what's shown in bold:

C:\>**STUP-PC\BUGLE\BUGLE 20 S**

The call selection 20 invokes BUGLE, and the letter S adds another argument to suppress the program's usual tendency to identify the call being played. "Taps" will then play without any identification of the cause!

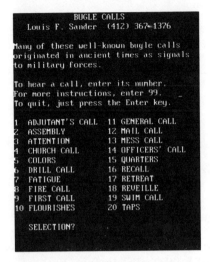

Figure 4. Bugle Calls:
BUGLE offers 20 bugle calls.

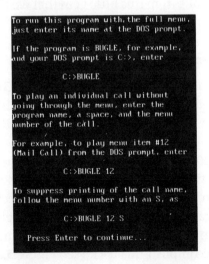

Figure 5. Bugle Help:
BUGLE even offers on-line help that teaches you how to play a specific call without stopping at the menu screen.

Escaping BUGLE

To quit, press <Enter>. BUGLE is a program, rather than a TSR, so it will not install itself in memory to haunt you (or your victim) later on. Once you quit, BUGLE will no longer consume any memory resources.

Suggestions for Using BUGLE

BUGLE's educational capabilities will be obvious to anyone who's ever had to learn the difference between the mouthpiece and the bell on a bugle, but its stupid applications are equally interesting.

As a file that gets executed every time a PC starts up, the AUTOEXEC.BAT file is an obvious candidate for the addition of lines such as the following. The parenthetical remarks are just that: Only the bold text should be included in an AUTOEXEC.BAT file.

CD C:\STUP-PC\BUGLE
BUGLE 18 S (plays "Reveille")
BUGLE 6 S (plays "Drill Call")
CD C:

By writing additional batch files for running certain applications, you can incorporate other bugle calls into your environment (or someone else's). A natural pairing is call number 12, "Mail Call," with an electronic mail application. (Note: We definitely don't recommend renaming mail applications for networked users who share a server-resident mail program.)

By renaming the user's electronic mail application and substituting a batch file with the same filename, you can force "Mail Call" to be played before actually invoking the mail program. For the following example, we'll assume it's named MAIL.EXE and that it will run unchanged if renamed to MMAIL.EXE:

1.   C:\MAIL>**RENAME MAIL.EXE MMAIL.EXE**
Changes the name of the mail program from MAIL to MMAIL.

2. Create the file MAIL.BAT with the contents:
   ECHO OFF   (turns off command echo)
   C:\STUP-PC\BUGLE\BUGLE 12 S
   MMAIL

3. Put MAIL.BAT in the directory where MAIL.EXE
   (now renamed to MMAIL.EXE) is normally
   found, for example:
   C:>**COPY MAIL.BAT C:\MAIL**

Since the user normally enters **MAIL** to invoke a mail utility, entering **MAIL** after these changes are made causes the MAIL.BAT file to execute, and makes "Mail Call" play before the mail application starts up.

In order for this to work properly, BUGLE has to be somewhere on the user's DOS PATH (for more information on the DOS PATH, see the glossary at the end of the book), or you must use a complete DOS filename for the program. (For example, in the directory structure created by the installation utility, STUPID.BAT, this would work the same as the previous steps indicate: **C:\STUP-PC\BUGLE\BUGLE 12 S**).

This technique will work for just about anything. Other pairings between bugle calls and applications will no doubt suggest themselves, so have fun!

BUGLE: The Fine Print

This version of BUGLE was lovingly put together by Louis F. Sander of Pittsburgh, Pennsylvania. He spent a good deal of time talking to us about the amount of research required to find the scores for all the bugle calls in the program. As it turns out, his best source of information was the director of the U.S. Navy band, who happened to have a set of antique recordings of many calls that would otherwise have faded into obscurity.

Mr. Sander sees BUGLE as a way of rescuing these bugle calls from oblivion, since even the military now uses recorded bugle calls on many posts, rather than employing a live bugler. It's not often that computer technology can help preserve a fading art, but in this case it may make a difference and provide some golden opportunities for stupidity at the same time.

This program is freeware, so feel free to share it with your friends and co-workers.

BUGLE: The Files

BUGLE includes one file:

BUGLE.EXE: The BUGLE program, with built-in operating instructions and documentation

FOOL

 "The world is but a fool's paradise..."

What FOOL Does

FOOL is a charming DOS irritant that pops up from time to time while you're entering data at the DOS prompt and insults you before executing the command you've just entered.

FOOL intercepts all keyboard input and deliberately or randomly responds with a remark to your screen. Here are a few of the remarks that can come up while you're busy working at the PC:

> "This is a stupid program."

> "Eat my shorts..."

> "Learn to splel, danmit!"

FOOL is one of those tricks that you'll find entertaining to use yourself, but it's even more fun to inflict it on other people. If you install it on some unsuspecting co-worker's machine and set the probability of a remark to very low (1% or 5%), it could be some time before he or she figures out what's going on. Rest assured, it's all good clean fun and won't do anything other than drive people crazy. On the other hand, you could lose your job. Or worse.

Most Stupid PC Tricks (let's call them SPCTs from now on) have limited appeal: They're funny at first, but after you've shown them to your friends and colleagues and have trapped all the unsuspecting or unwary, the tricks tend to lose their allure. You'll find yourself removing them from your normal executing environment and will quickly forget that they exist.

FOOL doesn't wear out as quickly as some other SPCTs, for a number of reasons. For one thing, the remarks file that FOOL draws from to send its messages to the screen is just a normal text file that you can change and edit to your heart's content; for another, if you turn the randomizer to a very low probability, it will remain enough of a novelty to stay fun rather than becoming a bore. If you take the effort to personalize the remarks file and to change the text, FOOL can stay fresh and entertaining for a long time.

How to Use FOOL

FOOL behaves like a TSR, a terminate-and-stay-resident program. This means that when you install FOOL, it becomes a part of your working environment at all times. This is necessary so that FOOL can stick around to insult you randomly or when you run certain programs.

Installing FOOL is easy, but remember, we're assuming that you've used STUPID.BAT to set up your SPCTs. The bold text is what you type in, and the comments that follow tell you what's going on:

1. **CD C:\STUP-PC\FOOL**

2. C:\STUP-PC\FOOL>**COPY FOOLISH. C:**
   Copies the remarks file to the root directory on C:\ (it must be somewhere on the DOS PATH in order for FOOL to work). It's even more fun if you first customize the FOOLISH file.

3. C:\STUP-PC\FOOL>**FOOL**
   Starts the FOOL program running (see the following information about parameters and associated values).

FOOL allows you to specify the randomness of its activity—that is, the percentage of the time it will interfere with normal DOS commands. Acceptable values for this percentage are 1, 5, 10, 25, 50, where 10 percent is the value that gets chosen for you if no value is supplied when FOOL is invoked. Notice that 100% is not an acceptable value. If you try to use 100% you will receive an error message.

If you want to make FOOL a part of your normal working environment (or someone else's), type the following to add these lines to the machine's AUTOEXEC.BAT file (remember to make a backup!):

CD C:\STUP-PC\FOOL

C:\STUP-PC\FOOL>**FOOL.EXE 1%**

CD C:

Don't forget that the remarks file, FOOLISH, has to be available somewhere on the DOS PATH. (For more information on the DOS PATH, see the glossary at the end of the book.) Also, please note that the percent sign (%) is not optional, but is required after the number to make FOOL work properly. The full DOS file specification is used to invoke the FOOL program (for example, C:\STUP-PC\FOOL\FOOL.EXE) on the assumption that you might not want to add that directory to your (or your victims') DOS PATH. Any change in the file's location will have to be reflected in the way it gets invoked in the AUTOEXEC.BAT file.

The FOOLISH (Remarks) File

FOOL reads its remarks and gets some of its instructions from the FOOLISH file. The first three lines of the file are especially interesting, because they make it possible for you to block certain commands from being executed altogether and to always be answered with a remark instead. The format for the first three lines is especially important, and these lines cannot be omitted. Here's a description of what the first three lines must look like:

program [optional program-specific message]

program [optional program-specific message]

program [optional program-specific message]

Substitute the name of a program for the word "program." For example, to disable WordPerfect and always reply with the remark, "Try a REAL word processor!", line 1 should be edited to read as follows:

WP Try a REAL word processor!

(Note: WP.EXE is the name of the file in which WordPerfect resides; it will be executed even if the .EXE extension is omitted. The Word Perfect directory must be after FOOL directory in the DOS PATH— for example: C:\;C:\STUP-PC\Fool;C:\WP50;...)

Specifying a remark is optional, but any time you specify a program name on any of the first three lines of the FOOLISH file, it will never execute (that's right, the program will not execute and the only response will be an insult). If a remark is not provided on lines 1–3, FOOL picks one at random from the other lines in the FOOLISH file.

If you'd rather not interfere with the machine's ability to run certain DOS programs, the first three lines in the FOOLISH file must be replaced with pound signs (#). If you want to make FOOL a part of your normal working environment, we suggest taking this route.

If you decide to install FOOL on a co-worker's machine and also decide to take advantage of its program-blocking abilities, we suggest that you stick around to watch what happens when your victim tries to run one of the blocked programs. You may have to bail your co-worker out of the fix so that he or she (and you) can get on with your work.

The rest of the FOOLISH file consists of some 40 remark lines. You can add to this collection, edit it, replace it with text of your own choice, or whatever. Each individual line in the file starting with line 4 is treated as a unit and will be displayed as a remark if chosen for display.

To edit FOOLISH., use the built-in DOS editor, EDLIN, or any other editor that can handle text only (ASCII) files. If you use a word processor, be sure to save the file as text only, sometimes called "pure ASCII."

A word of warning: The author elected to build a "profanity filter" into FOOL, so be warned that most four-letter words will be censored by the program and won't ever get displayed (besides, it's a lot more fun to think of creative euphemisms than to use those nasty words directly). There is some latitude as to what's permitted, however. Figure 6, *Foolin' Around,* shows the results of entering the names of three bogus programs (ack, nack, and quack) entered as the first three lines of the FOOLISH file, along with the message that FOOL displays when it's already installed ("I'm here...").

Escaping FOOL

As a TSR-like program, FOOL will stick around until it's explicitly removed from the DOS environment. The easiest way to get rid of it is to reboot your machine. Remember, however, that if FOOL is in the AUTOEXEC.BAT file, it will restart with everything else. If you have added the FOOL command to the AUTOEXEC.BAT file, remove the FOOL reference before rebooting, or you'll be right back where you started.

You can also remove TSRs after you have installed them, if you have the right software utilities to make this happen. See Appendix A, "Managing TSRs," for instructions about using a tool to get rid of FOOL (or any other TSR that you might want to get rid of).

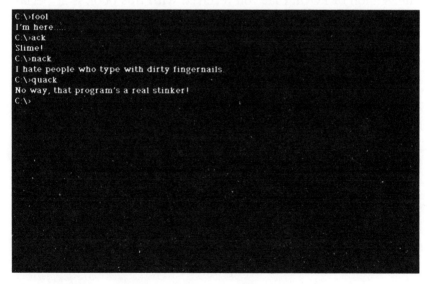

```
C:\>fool
I'm here....
C:\>ack
Slime!
C:\>nack
I hate people who type with dirty fingernails.
C:\>quack
No way, that program's a real stinker!
C:\>
```

Figure 6. Foolin' Around:
Fool talks back, no matter what you type at the DOS prompt.

Suggestions for Using FOOL

FOOL is one of a few SPCTs that you may want to make a part of your normal working environment. If you decide to install it as a part of your AUTOEXEC.BAT file, we suggest that you put pound signs (#) in the first three lines of the FOOLISH file so that the program does not interfere with normal working conditions. It's also a good idea to keep the probability low that FOOL will issue a remark (we recommend 1% or 5%).

In tormenting others, you have to decide if you want to block their access to certain programs (we think that's a bad idea, because doing so can stop people from being able to do their jobs). Be sure to get a backup of their AUTOEXEC.BAT file, or be ready to step in and help them get back to a normal environment once the fun is over. Also, be prepared to deal with the consequences of inflicting this irresponsibly on others—you may not be the only person to buy this book, and there are other ways to get revenge here, too!

FOOL: The Fine Print

The version of FOOL that you received with this book is a special, rewritten version that the author, Dan Desjardins, provided for our use (and uploaded to CompuServe). This program is shareware, and the author requests a $5.00 registration fee (a "pittance," as he calls it) if you like this program.

If you do like the program, send a check or money order to Dan Desjardins, 6426 Hubbard Ave., Middleton, WI 53562. We conclude with Dan's closing lines to his .DOC file: "heh heh!"

FOOL: The Files

The FOOL program includes the following files:

FOOL.DOC	The documentation file for FOOL; worth reading if you want to learn more about the program
FOOL.EXE	The FOOL program

FOOLISH   The remarks file (This file must
                   be somewhere on the DOS
                   PATH for FOOL to work. For
                   more information on the DOS
                   PATH, see the glossary at the
                   end of the book.)

MUTANT

 "The Ghost in the Machine"

What MUTANT Does

MUTANT is a program that adds an element of mystery to any PC. It makes your computer sound as if it is possessed by a demon that manifests itself as anything from a hyperactive squirrel to a caffeine-crazed blackbird. In some cases, it sounds as if the bearings on the hard disk are starting to fail and can induce some interesting states of panic in unknowing users, including machine disassembly or expensive service calls.

How to Use MUTANT

MUTANT is another TSR; once installed, it will do its thing until stopped. Because it can be kind of irritating, we don't recommend that you put it into anybody's AUTOEXEC.BAT file (if you do, remember to edit that file when the time comes for MUTANT to disappear). MUTANT takes only one file and one command to run, so it can be fired off at a moment's notice. You don't even have to copy the file over to somebody else's machine to make the program work; it can be executed from a floppy on the sly, and its recipient will never be the wiser.

MUTANT can be started up from just about anywhere, as long as the file is present on the current DOS PATH (for more information on the DOS PATH, see the glossary at the end of the book), or you can use an explicit DOS reference:

C:\> **C:\STUP-PC\MUTANT\MUTANT**

Once MUTANT has been installed, it will take a short while (one to two minutes at most) for the beast within the computer to start attempting its escape. At this point, all you have to do is to sit back and enjoy the reaction.

Our beta testers found that MUTANT does not work well on some older PCs, especially 8088 CPUs (PC/XTs). It's best to avoid running MUTANT on these machines. If you have an older PC and still want to try MUTANT, we urge you to proceed with caution.

Escaping MUTANT

Since MUTANT is a TSR, the basic technique for removal is to reboot the machine by pressing <Ctrl>-<Alt>-<Del> (as long as MUTANT isn't hiding in the AUTOEXEC.BAT file). It can also be removed from the DOS environment with the TSR management utilities discussed in Appendix A, "Managing TSRs."

Suggestions for Using MUTANT

MUTANT is a sonic enhancement to your PC environment: Once you start MUTANT up, it will stick around and make strange noises as long as you can stand them. If not played as a trick on others, we recommend that you use it directly—that is by invoking the MUTANT program at the DOS keyboard. This way, you can rid yourself of the infamous "squirrel-bird" any time you want simply by restarting your machine (or somebody else's machine, if that's where it's running). For the same reasons, we don't recommend calling it from the AUTOEXEC.BAT file.

MUTANT: The Fine Print

MUTANT was written by John Millington as a learning exercise to practice writing TSRs with a brand new C compiler (he includes the source code with the program materials for the terminally curious). His goal was to create some background sound effects that could happen while other work is going on, without unduly disturbing one's work environment. He's right about another thing, too: MUTANT makes its most horrifying appearance on older, slower PCs as if to prove that they may be old, but not obsolete. John doesn't ask for donations, but you can contact him at 5577 Wyoming Blvd. NE, #314N, Albuquerque, NM 87109.

MUTANT: The Files

The MUTANT program includes the following files:

MUTANT.C:	The original C source code for MUTANT
MUTANT.EXE:	The executable MUTANT program
MUTREAD.ME:	MUTANT's brief, but amusing, documentation

MLPUSH

 "Go ahead, push your luck!"

What MLPUSH Does

MLPUSH is a dice game that you can play with the computer, with other players, or both (see Figure 7, *MLPUSH Main Screen*). It is a fast-moving game in which players try to use a modicum of strategy and as much luck as possible to run up the highest score. MLPUSH is based on an old dice game called Drop Dead, with a few embellishments added by its author to improve the fun.

How to Use MLPUSH

MLPUSH will run on just about any PC or compatible and is capable of supporting additional features, such as a Microsoft-compatible mouse, fast-mode operation, and both color and monochrome displays. It also keeps a Top Ten Scores file, presents statistics on multiple games, and supports a very important feature for addicted gamesters, the "BossKey," which presents a phony DOS-prompt screen that you can use when someone in authority comes by.

Running the program is easy: Simply enter the program name, MLPUSH, at the DOS prompt (**C:\STUP-PC\MLPUSH\MLPUSH**). The following table presents the commands available in the program alphabetically:

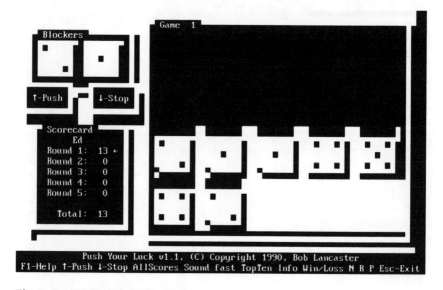

Figure 7. MLPUSH Main Screen:
MLPUSH is a dice game that requires strategy and luck.

Key	Key Label/Explanation
A	Allscores command: Presents a scorecard for all players to permit scores to be compared (see Figure 8, *Allscores*).
B	BossKey command: Displays a phony DOS screen to keep players looking productive. Entering **OK** at the "DOS" prompt restores the game in play.
\<Esc\>	Exit command: Exits MLPUSH and returns to DOS.
F	Fast mode: Plays the game without dice animation or other visual frills or sounds.
I	Program info: Shows information about the program and its author.
N	Next Prompt toggle: Toggles prompting for the next player message on and off.
P	Pips Mode: Toggles between selecting dice with pips (dots) or dice with numbers on their faces.

R	Round Prompt toggle: Toggles the message with the round number at the beginning of each round.
S	Sound Mode toggle: Turns game sounds on and off, as desired. (Fast mode also turns off the sound.)
T	Top Ten scores: Shows the ten highest scores registered on your machine to date (stored in the file MLPUSH.SCR). After being displayed, the Top Ten scores can be cleared by pressing <Alt>-C.
W	Win/Loss Statistics: Shows stats for all games played in the current session. While always shown at the end of each game, this command lets you call stats up at any time.

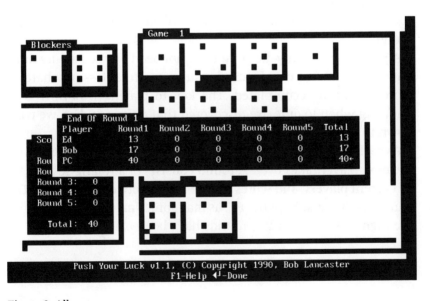

Figure 8. Allscores:
Pressing the A key at any time shows all players' scores.

You can enter the commands in the previous table at any time during a game to control the program's behavior. The following options can be entered on the command line only when MLPUSH is being invoked (you cannot change them once the program is running):

Key	Explanation
B	Black-and-White mode: Forces MLPUSH to run in black and white.
M	Mouse: If a mouse driver is installed and you don't want to use the mouse, this option will suppress the mouse from having an effect on the game.
T	Top Ten Scores: Controls whether or not the scores get saved at all; intended to make operation from a write-protected disk possible.

After all these operational details, playing the game itself is remarkably simple: The computer rolls two dice, which act as blockers (any dice that show up with the same value cannot be counted toward the total score, nor rolled again during a single round).

A player can roll any dice that have not been blocked at any time, but getting all five dice blocked results in a total loss of whatever score has been accumulated. The key to playing MLPUSH is in knowing when to quit (we discovered that quitting when we were down to two dice remaining was the wisest course).

As each player voluntarily or involuntarily gives up his or her turn, the next player takes over. A round consists of a rolling session for all current players, and scores are presented between each turn. The winner is the person (or the PC, as may sometimes be the case) with the highest score after five rounds have been played out.

Escaping MLPUSH

Getting out of MLPUSH is very easy: The current player can press <Esc> at any time, which causes a dialog box to appear that asks, "Exit Push Your Luck?" Pressing **Y** will end the program and leave behind an information screen. The <Ctrl>-C key combination does not work to exit MLPUSH, but you can use <Ctrl>-<Break>. We recommend that you use the <Esc> key because exiting with <Ctrl>-<Break> will leave the screen filled with the the MLPUSH display in use at the time of exit. If you must use <Ctrl>-<Break> to exit, follow this with the DOS CLS (Clear Screen) command to clear up the wreckage.

There's also a temporary "escape" from MLPUSH, built to keep real addicts out of trouble. It's author calls it the "BossKey" or the "SpouseKey," and it suspends the game and temporarily displays a bogus DOS prompt so that it looks like you're really working to a casual observer (any commands come back with errors, so it won't stand real scrutiny). Pressing **B** any time during play calls up this bogus DOS prompt; typing **OK** restores the game.

Suggestions for Using MLPUSH

Use MLPUSH quietly (sound off), quickly (fast display option), and as often as you can get away with it! It's delightfully addictive, but eminently playable, thanks to the BossKey (don't forget, its alternate name is the SpouseKey, which is appropriate for the authors).

MLPUSH: The Fine Print

MLPUSH was written by Bob Lancaster, a mandolinist, pogonotrapher, and independent contract programmer living in the Los Angeles area with his wife Cindy and their three children: Rosamund, Genevieve, and Nathaniel. In his "spare time," Bob has written a series of well-received shareware computer games.

MLPUSH is a shareware program, with a suggested donation of $5.00 (well worth it, in our humble opinions). As long as the .DOC file travels with the program, you can share it freely with colleagues and friends. Mr. Lancaster's address is P.O. Box 5612, Hacienda Heights, CA 91745.

MLPUSH: The Files

MLPUSH includes two files and creates a third:

MLPUSH.DOC:	The MLPUSH documentation file (worth reading)
MLPUSH.EXE	The MLPUSH program
MLPUSH.SCR	The Top Ten Scores file, created and maintained by MLPUSH once the program is run

GR

 "Graphics zip for most display types"

What GR Does

GR is a program that creates and displays random, two-dimensional figures until interrupted. It uses a Spirograph-like plotting technique (see Figure 9, *Like a Spirograph*) to create figures from one of six basic plot types and will work on monochrome or color displays of the following types: CGA, EGA, and VGA. It will *not* work with a Hercules display.

In monochrome environments, GR plots a continuing succession of line plots, making it an effective screen blanker. GR doesn't have anywhere near as much appeal in a monochrome environment as it does in a color environment, where each line in a plot gets drawn in a slightly different color as the program works its way through the color palette.

How to Use GR

All that's necessary to set GR in motion is to call the program by name, as long as it's available on your DOS PATH. (For more information on the DOS PATH, see the glossary at the end of the book.) To run GR, type **C:\STUP-PC\GR\GR**.

Figure 9. Like a Spirograph:
GR generates beautiful, Spirograph-like images. It looks best on a color monitor.

Escaping GR

Pressing <Enter> is the preferred method for exiting GR, but almost any key will do the job. We recommend using <Enter> or <Return> to exit GR, because they behave most reliably across the various environments tested.

We recommend avoiding traditional DOS escapes, such as <Ctrl>-C or <Ctrl>-<Break>, because they will leave the screen showing the most recent GR figure. This type of bailout can cause further problems on a color monitor, because it will not reset the display to its default mode. If you have to use a bailout, remember the DOS Clear Screen command—CLS—and learn how to reset your display, if necessary.

Suggestions for Using GR

GR makes an effective screen blanker, both for color and mono-chrome environments. It keeps your screen in motion and thereby extends the life of your display. We recommend using it whenever you take a break from your machine, but have to leave it running for whatever reason (in some companies, it's forbidden to turn machines off because cycling the on-off switch is the most likely time for a system to fail).

The program's author recommends a 12 MHz or faster AT machine for this program (he claims that performance is "almost unbearable" on an XT machine). Because the program can benefit from access to a math coprocessor, we can only speculate that GR spends most of its processing time crunching numbers to figure out where to plot its figures. That is why a faster machine is better. It is also why a math coprocessor will make a difference.

GR: The Fine Print

GR was developed by Paul Schaefer, a programmer based in Troy, Michigan. It is freeware and may be shared with colleagues, coworkers, and other DOS enthusiasts. The source code for the program, written in Microsoft C, is also included for those incurable hackers who might want to tinker further with their displays.

GR: The Files

GR includes the following files:

GR.C	Microsoft C Version 5.1 source for GR
GR.DOC	Brief documentation file
GR.EXE	GR program

TRIP

 "Mind-bending changes to the DOS display"

What TRIP Does

TRIP is probably the purest manifestation of a prototypical SPCT. It was written specifically as a practical joke to mess with a fellow PC user's mind. TRIP randomly selects a character on the screen and replaces that character with one just like it, except in a different color. On monochrome screens, the effect is equally interesting: It makes characters randomly fade or disappear altogether.

The overall effect is that a demon is loose behind your PC's display, causing all kinds of changes and apparent motion on the screen. It is especially bothersome in areas where you're not currently focused, and it will drive your peripheral vision crazy, literally forcing your eyes to jump around the screen.

How to Use TRIP

Because TRIP is a TSR program, it stays in place forevermore once started up. In addition to requiring that you type in the name of the program (TRIP), it also expects to be fed a number, which corresponds to the number of milliseconds between color changes. Any number between 1 and 1000 seems to work, although as the number gets higher, TRIP's effects become much subtler and harder to detect. (See Figure 10, *Taking a Trip*.)

61

```
randomly select a character on the screen and replace that
characters color with a random color.


Disclaimer - I claim no responsibility for any damage
             resulting from the use of TRIP.


Usage:  C:\TRIP <number>

     <number> - This is where you specify the delay you want
                between color changes.


   If you enjoy this program and would like to see more
programs of this sort, please send me a letter with ideas or
leave me mail on GEnie.  If leaving me mail on GEnie
please send it to:  P.BINDER.  And, "Thank you for your
support."

                       Peter S. Binder
                       GEnie: P.BINDER
```

Figure 10. Taking a Trip:
TRIP replaces a character's color with random colors; the delay between color changes is user-specified.

As TSR's go, TRIP is not especially well-behaved: It will allow multiple copies of itself to be loaded, making it possible to mess up your lower 640 KB of working DOS memory, unless you're really careful. If you try to change the speed by typing **TRIP** followed by a number, it loads an additional copy of the program instead of changing the speed of the copy that's already running. Forewarned is forearmed.

Despite these minor drawbacks, TRIP is an excellent SPCT, and it makes for some interesting-looking displays, particularly on color monitors, where it looks like someone with a perverted color sense has gone crazy behind the screen.

Escaping TRIP

Because TRIP is a TSR, removing it from a working DOS environment requires the use of special TSR management tools (for more information see Appendix A, "Managing TSRs"). Alternatively, you can remove TRIP from a DOS environment using the traditional "three-fingered salute"—that is, rebooting by pressing <Ctrl>-<Alt>-<Del> simultaneously.

Some system crashes prevent the keyboard from being recognized. In the unlikely event that the machine won't even respond to the "salute," it may be necessary to turn it off and then turn it back on (this problem did not crop up during our testing). There's nothing you can do to prevent this from happening, but if the salute goes unrecognized, remember to turn off your machine and then turn it back on again.

Suggestions for Using TRIP

The author's intention of building the materials for a practical joke remains TRIP's best application. Because it is so distracting, we strongly recommend against including it in someone's AUTOEXEC.BAT file (especially your own). This program is best launched from a floppy right from the victim's keyboard (for example, C:\>**A:\TRIP 5**), followed by the CLS (Clear Screen) command to remove any evidence from the victim's display, or type **C:\STUP-PC\TRIP\TRIP 5**.

You might want to keep a copy handy on your own hard drive to amuse passers-by or other random visitors, but make sure you work out a strategy for removing TRIP when you get tired of it. It is almost impossible to get any work done with this TSR running on your desktop.

TRIP: The Fine Print

TRIP was written by Peter S. Binder of Snoqualmie, Washington. It is freeware and may be shared with colleagues, co-workers, and other prospective victims. Peter does not request donations for TRIP, but he does welcome comments and suggestions for other software. You can write him at 40612 SE 60th Street, Snoqualmie, WA 98065.

With an obviously creative and dangerously warped mind like his, you'd better beware of requesting something really heinous—it's liable to show up on your machine without an invitation.

TRIP: The Files

TRIP includes the following files:

TRIP.DOC	A one-page description of TRIP
TRIP.EXE	The TRIP TSR program

SSB

 "Long may it wave!"

What SSB Does

Expanding the acronym tells the story. SSB stands for Star-Spangled Banner, and that's just what this program does: It plays the National Anthem—all four verses—without stopping. Before we found this little gem, we didn't even know that our anthem *had* four verses, let alone all the words for verses two through four (see Figure 11, *SSB's Second Verse*).

This program is just plain fun and is a must-have for all you true-blue patriots out there. As a diversion, it's fun to watch SSB do its thing. As an irritant, it's magnificent to force your compatriots (pun intended) to waste their time waiting for the song to play to completion. It's especially vexing if you jump to attention when it begins playing and salute the screen, while haranguing them to do the same.

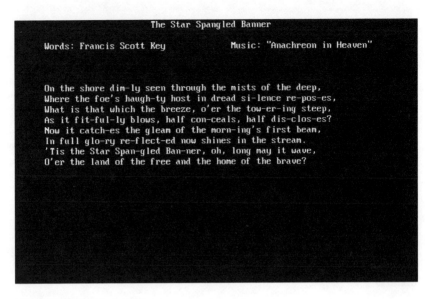

Figure 11. SSB's Second Verse:
"On the shore dim-ly seen..."

How to Use SSB

Using SSB couldn't be simpler. All you have to do is execute the SSB program by typing **C:\STUP-PC\SSB\SSB**. It is best viewed on a color screen, because it can be instructed (with the F2 function key) to take advantage of color and highlight each word in the song as it's being played. On a monochrome CRT, it can highlight the word (depending on the display type); on a gas plasma display, it doesn't appear to be highlighting along at all.

When you start SSB up, it presents the screen depicted in Figure 12, *SSB Startup Screen*. This screen provides some controls using various function keys, as indicated in the following table:

Key	Key Label/Explanation
F1	Monochrome text: Tells SSB that you have a mono-chrome text display. Causes the song to play.

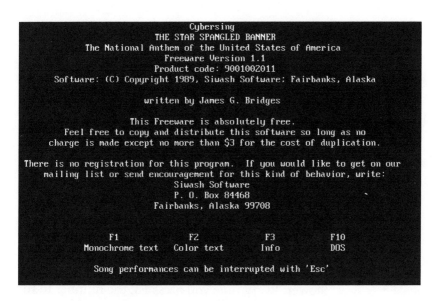

Figure 12. SSB Start-up Screen:
The screen you'll see when you first start SSB.

F2   Color text: Tells SSB you have a color display (to SSB, any monochrome display—CGA, EGA, VGA, and so on—is a monochrome text display). Pressing F2 makes no difference for anything but real color. Causes the song to play.

F3   Info: A one-screen background on the "Star-Spangled Banner," focused on the events at Ft. Henry that inspired F. Scott Key to write it. Striking any key returns to the start-up screen.

F10   DOS: Returns to the DOS prompt (terminates the SSB program).

Once you've had a chance to play around with F3 once or twice, that option will quickly lose its appeal. F10 gives you one last chance to bail out on your patriotic duty before playing the Anthem, so F1 and F2 are where the red, white, and blue action is. Try to pick the function key that matches your display, but don't worry: SSB doesn't care, it'll play the song either way on almost any kind of display.

Once it's playing, you can use <Esc> to control SSB's behavior, as follows. Pressing <Esc> causes the following function keys to be documented in a menu that appears at the base of the screen displaying the current verse being played.

Key	Key Label/Explanation
F1	Play song: Starts the tune going at the current speed setting.
F2	Faster: A number to the right of F2 on the screen increases by 1 every time you press F2 (the default setting is 10). As the number gets higher, the song plays faster (and starts losing musical details—try it set to 199 for a good laugh).
F3	Slower: Every time you press F3, the number to the left decreases by 1. As the number gets lower, the song plays more slowly (for an appreciation of the phrase "geological time," try it set to 2 or 3).
	The speed setting for SSB is displayed as a whole number between the top menu line (that is, between the F2 and F3 key names).
F4	Color: Starts over but acts as if you have a color monitor (works only on a color monitor, so in most cases this acts as a restart button).
F5	Recycle: Causes the song to be repeated indefinitely until you press <Esc>. Use this only in emergencies—it'll drive you crazy! This key is a toggle—if you press it twice, it cancels the recycle instruction.
F9	Main: Returns to the start-up screen (see Figure 12).
F10	DOS: Returns to the DOS prompt (terminates the SSB program).

Escaping SSB

While the music is playing, press <Esc>, and then press F10 to return to the DOS prompt.

Suggestions for Using SSB

There's no way to inflict SSB on someone else without their cooperation (F10 will always allow them to escape back to DOS), so it's best to make it participatory. It's a neat demonstration of the PC's basic musical capabilities and can be used as a "Hey, listen to this!" attention grabber. Our kids really love SSB and were as interested to see verses 2 through 4 as we were.

If you must play (and who mustn't?), varying the speed of SSB can produce some pretty hilarious results, especially when you speed it up.

SSB: The Fine Print

SSB was programmed by James G. Bridges of Siwash Software in Fairbanks, Alaska. He welcomes your feedback and, and if you'd like to get on Siwash Software's mailing list, be sure to include your name and address. If this program is any indication of the kind of work that Siwash can do, getting on the mailing list would be a good idea. The address is Siwash Software, P.O. Box 84468, Fairbanks, AK 99708-4468.

SSB: The Files

SSB includes just one file:

SSB.EXE:	The SSB program. The featured performance of our National Anthem, "The Star-Spangled Banner"

ADULATE

 "The program that panders to your ego!"

What ADULATE Does

ADULATE is a program that responds to a request for a comment by replying with a cheerful and blatant compliment to its caller. Its author describes the program best in his lead-in paragraph of the accompanying .DOC file:

> *"In this rat-race of a world it [is] good to have someone (or even something) that you can rely on for a bit of obsequious grovelling. So, if you haven't got any sycophantic minions, you can use this program to force your poor, unsuspecting PC to bolster your ego. Call it from your AUTOEXEC.BAT for a cringing start to the day's computing, or type **ADU-LATE 20** for a boost during a really bad session. You'll soon be on top of the world again!"*

ADULATE can be a refreshing change from one's usual interactions with the computer. Given some of the dirtier tricks we've suggested that you might play on your colleagues or co-workers, you might want to keep ADULATE in reserve as a way of getting back into their good graces later on.

How to Use ADULATE

ADULATE reads a special file, called ADULATE.FMT, to generate its compliments. In order for ADULATE to work properly, the ADULATE.FMT file has to be in your current working directory. This means, for instance, that if you want to make a call to ADULATE a part of your AUTOEXEC.BAT file, as the author suggests, you have to copy ADULATE.FMT into your root directory.

In fact, here's the script for a short batch file that assumes that ADULATE.FMT has been copied into the root directory and that the ADULATE program, ADULATE.EXE, is available somewhere on your DOS PATH. (For more information on the DOS PATH, see the glossary at the end of the book.) It requires you to provide the full path of your current directory (to return you to where you started) so that you can continue where you left off after turning to ADU-LATE for a bit of consolation or encouragement.

Let's call this batch file ADUL.BAT (as usual, enter only the bold text when creating the file):

ECHO OFF	(Turns off command echo)
CD C:	(Change directory to root)
ADULATE 2	(Display two compliments)
CD %1	(Change directory to value of supplied string)

Here's how you'd use it once you defined it. Let's assume your current directory is C:\WORK\LTR and that ADUL.BAT is available on your DOS PATH. To call ADUL.BAT to return you to that directory when it finished, you'd enter the string **ADUL C:\WORK\LTR**. This will go off to the root directory, write a couple of compliments to the screen, and return to where you started.

For those in need of an extra boost, supplying a number after the ADULATE program name will result in said number of compliments being supplied. Our batch file includes the line **ADULATE 2**; this causes the program to display two compliments. Depending on the format, between 18 and 22 compliments typically fill an entire screen, so that number is an effective limit to the number of compliments worth asking for at any one time. You can ask for more, but chances are that they'll scroll by before you can read them.

Escaping ADULATE

ADULATE is a program that responds to your invocation with one or more effusively complimentary remarks (by default, it responds with one compliment only). For small numbers of compliments, the program is faster than your fingers: You won't be able to tell it to quit before it's already finished.

Should you instruct ADULATE to stroke you with large numbers of compliments (say, five or more), bailing out when sycophantic overload strikes is very easy: Entering <Ctrl>-C or <Ctrl>-<Break> will immediately stop the program and return you to the DOS prompt. Because ADULATE is a character-oriented program that doesn't do funny things to the screen, this is entirely safe and won't cause any subsequent display problems.

Editing the ADULATE.FMT File

The author supplies four formats for adulatory remarks in the ADULATE.FMT file, but he very kindly also provides a set of rules for adding to or changing that file (see Figure 13, *Remarkable Adulations*, for the contents of the ADULATE.FMT file). The compliments he supplies are interesting, but a little work on your part will result in a custom compliment environment (in fact, you could even make your successes at editing this environment the subject of one or more compliments).

The key ingredients in the ADULATE.FMT file depicted in Figure 13 are the "%s" entries that occur in each line. These entries signal ADULATE to scan its internal list of adjectives and nouns, and randomly select a particular word to replace the %s string. Each line begins with an uppercase "F" to indicate that it will be used as a part of a specific compliment format (you can run ADULATE without a corresponding ADULATE.FMT file, but the results are far less interesting).

```
C:\>type test\adulate.fmt
FCompuServe is the %s %s of the %s %s\n
FHail, o %s %s of the %s %s\n
FWhat is your wish, %s %s of the %s %s?\n
FRegards from Larry Cobb to the %s %s of the %s %s\n

C:\>
```

Figure 13. Remarkable Adulations:
A template for generating your own adulatory remarks.

It's a good idea to specify %s values in pairs so that an adjective-noun phrase will be randomly selected by ADULATE. ADULATE always provides words as adjective, noun, adjective, noun, and so on; specifying only a single %s will cause either an adjective or a noun to display, depending on what ADULATE displayed last.

You'll need to edit ADULATE.FMT with an ASCII-only editor or to remove any special characters (ASCII values higher than 127) from the ADULATE.FMT file before using it. Otherwise, it won't behave properly.

ADULATE.FMT supports the same type of output control that the C language "printf" statement recognizes. If you are unfamiliar with this notation, refer to the following table to see what ADULATE recognizes and how it causes the output to behave.

Parameter	Definition	Explanation
\b	backspace (BS)	Backs up one space in the output file.
\f	form feed (FF)	New page printer command.
\n	new line (NL or LF)	Starts a new line.
\r	carriage return (CR)	Drops one line lower.
\t	tab (HT)	Skips to the next tab mark.
\\	double slash	Outputs one slash mark.

Unfortunately, our testing shows that on some machines the \r and \b format strings don't behave as one would expect them to. We suggest that you stay away from using these as well as \f because they are intended to control output to printers, not to your display screen. The others appear to work just fine, however.

Suggestions for Using ADULATE

The author's suggestion to add ADULATE to your AUTOEXEC.BAT file is worth considering, especially if you want to start the day with an effusive compliment. We've also provided a simple .BAT file that you can use to refresh yourself with a compliment at any time.

Because ADULATE is a DOS program (not a TSR), no special instructions are needed to manage it, other than what we've provided here and the information in the author's .DOC file.

As for inflicting ADULATE on others, the same batch file technique that we discussed in the chapter on FOOL will work to make a compliment mandatory before the user invokes a particular program. Using ADULATE on someone could be a way to restore yourself to the good graces of those upon whom you've inflicted other, less complimentary tricks.

ADULATE: The Fine Print

ADULATE is the brainchild of Larry Cobb (that's why he sends his compliments in one of the remarks in the ADULATE.FMT file), who uploaded his file all the way from the U.K. ADULATE is a public domain program by Larry T. Cobb Associates (CompuServe ID 100016,421). As long as the copyright notice is retained and the .DOC file is kept with the program, it can be freely distributed.

ADULATE: The Files

The following files are part of ADULATE:

ADULATE.DOC	The documentation file for ADULATE
ADULATE.EXE	The ADULATE program
ADULATE.FMT	The formats for ADULATE's compliments

PARAscan

 "If they're REALLY out to get you, it's not paranoia!"

What PARAscan Does

What PARAscan does is hilarious and priceless: It imitates a virus detection and correction utility, very convincingly at first. It's only when things get a little bit further into the program that a victim might begin to notice his or her leg being pulled, but after the second virus "fight scene," it's obvious to everybody that laughter is the only medicine that PARAscan can provide. (As an example, Figure 14, *PARA-abnormal*, shows a couple of PARAscan's tongue-in-cheek screens.)

Even when the joke's been discovered, there's still plenty of enjoyment left in the PARAscan, as it discovers and deals with ever more outrageous "virus infections." The following table shows a few of the mythical viruses that PARAscan describes:

ABC NEWS VIRUS   Spreads false data around on
                          your system.

GUMBY VIRUS   Makes crude, vulgar, insulting
                          remarks through the PC
                          speaker.

LORD SATAN VIRUS	Makes chips come alive and walk off.
GERALD R. FORD VIRUS	Predecessor of Dan Quayle virus.
SHROUD OF TURIN VIRUS	Creates an image of Jesus on the screen.

Don't worry, we haven't spoiled all the fun. There are many more viruses than we've documented here, and the program has to be run in order to be properly savored.

How to Use PARAscan

Running PARAscan is as easy as typing the program name in at the DOS prompt (i.e., **C:\STUP-PC\PARASCAN\PARASCAN**). As long as the program's somewhere on your DOS PATH, all you have to do is sit back and watch the fun! (For more information on the DOS PATH, see the glossary at the end of the book.)

Escaping PARAscan

If you need to exit PARAscan at any time, all you need to do is press <Return> or <Enter> (almost any key will do, actually). If you want to watch the whole thing go by, the program will end itself after about two or three minutes. We don't recommend using normal DOS bailouts (<Ctrl>-C or <Ctrl>-<Break>) to exit the program, because they will leave your screen littered with graphical remnants of the PARAscan program.

Suggestions for Using PARAscan

This is one of those SPCT's that cries out for an audience—preferably an uninformed one. As a "dirty trick," you could install it on someone else's machine, explaining the move with a need to "check their machine for the Jerusalem-B virus." Even under those auspices, it will quickly become obvious that you're having them on.

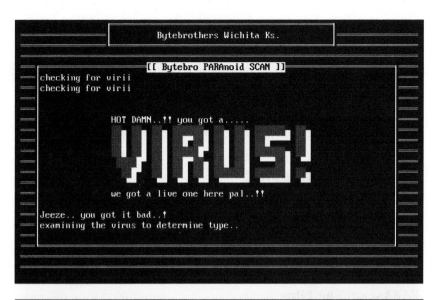

Figure 14. PARA-abnormal :
PARAscan's screens make it semi-obvious that your leg is being pulled.

Our preferred strategy is to show PARAscan off on our own machine, with a prefatory remark such as, "Have you seen this wild new virus checker I just got?" This invariably elicits a "ho-hum, if I have to" kind of reaction, but it quickly turns into laughter when the program starts doing its thing.

This is one of the more benign SPCTs and by far one of the most amusing.

PARAscan: The Fine Print

This program is the work of Jimmy Pearson, written under his company name, the Bytebrothers. It is freeware and is released with no charge or registration fee, so it can be shared with whomever you wish.

PARAscan: The Files

PARAscan includes two files:

PARASCAN.DOC	The PARAnoid SCANning system documentation
PARASCAN.EXE	The PARAnoid SCANning system program

Spiroplot

 "A popular toy makes its way to the PC"

What Spiroplot Does

Spiroplot is a computerized version of the popular Spirograph (a trademark of Kenner products), where complex designs get plotted with three wheels within a circular frame. Two of these wheels are movable, but the third is fixed, so the motion of the two free wheels is what produces the patterns that get traced onto the page (one or both wheels can be used to produce a plot, yielding more or less complex figures).

The program's author, Donald MacFarlane, was quick to realize that having the computer imitate the motion of the mechanical wheels in the original toy was an easy way to build and plot mathematical models. His approach was to implement the same kind of capability in a computer program and let the computer do all the work.

The automation of the plotting process adds one other significant benefit: The program has been set up to be driven by a file of wheel settings so that tracings can be created one after another, in sequence.

The author includes a large set of spiroplots in a file called SPIRO.DEM (includes 59 displays) that provides an excellent demonstration of the program's capabilities as well as great way to fill your screen up with an ever-changing flow of hypnotic images (his use of color isn't bad either, for those of you with color monitors). The demonstration keeps repeating after making its way through the entire set, so it makes an effective screen blanker.

How to Use SPIROPLOT

SPIROPLOT is a program that offers users the ability to set up their own traces or to execute existing trace files (SPIRO.DEM). To run the program, type

CD C:\STUP-PC\SPIRO

SPIRO

at the C:\> prompt. Figure 15, *SpiroPlots*, shows two of a wide variety of plots that the program can produce (unfortunately, we can't reproduce them in color, but even in black-and-white the images are gorgeous). The demonstration file (SPIRO.DEM) is useful for more than entertainment: Comparing the specifications for the graphs with the resulting plots helps a user understand how the program works. To read these specifications, print the demo file by entering **print C:\STUP-PC\SPIRO\SPIRO.DEM** at the C:\> prompt.

The Spiroplot Control Screen

Figure 16, *SpiroControls*, depicts the program's main menu from which all other activities are coordinated. The top menu bar (Window 1) contains the major activities supported by the program, while the remaining windows (2–4) are used to control how the program behaves (fixed, inside, and outside wheel controls) and whether or not Spiroplot displays the wheels while tracing its plots.

Note that this program uses a cursor that appears at the top of the character box on the screen, rather than at the bottom (as is more common with most DOS programs).

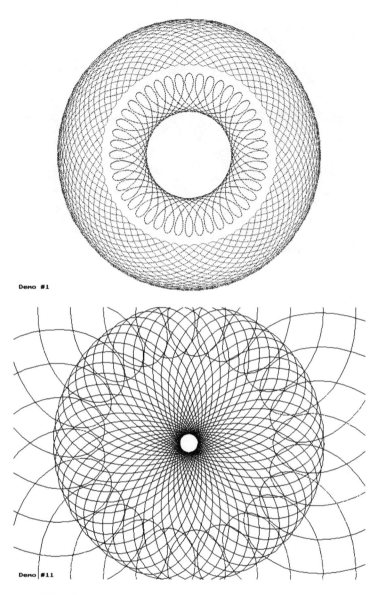

Figure 15. SpiroPlots:
Spiroplot, the computerized version of the Kenner Spirograph, creates complex
drawings using a set of simple controls.

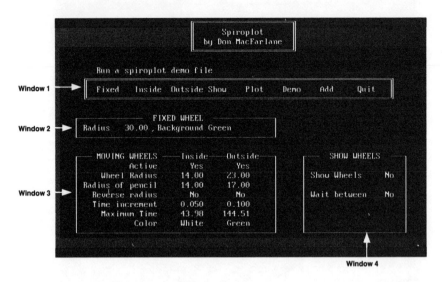

Window 1

Window 2

Window 3

Window 4

Figure 16. SpiroControls:
Spiroplot offers a wide range of choices for tracing plots.

Window 1 supports a range of choices, as documented in the following table.

Option	Explanation
Fixed	Sets the radius of the fixed wheel and the background color (black for monochrome; displayed in Window 2).
Inside	Selects the inside moving wheel and its associated parameters (displayed in Window 3, center column).
Outside	Selects the outside moving wheel and its associated parameters (also displayed in Window 3, rightmost column).
Show	Shows the wheel positions while drawing the spiroplot (the settings are displayed in Window 4). Makes the plotting process easier to follow and understand but slows it down somewhat.

84

Plot	Plots the spiroplot using the currently selected wheels and associated parameters.
Demo	Runs a spiroplot demo file (the default name is SPIRO.DEM).
Add	Adds a plot to a demo file (supply file name, or default is SPIRO.DEM).
Quit	Exits the Spiroplot program.

Overall, the program is easy to use and understand. It is a favorite with younger kids, because it produces interesting pictures with a minimum of effort (no real mathematical understanding of what's going on appears to be needed).

There is one important limitation to Spiroplot: It requires a graphics card of some kind (the range of supported types is broad, however, as indicated by the list of driver files listed under "Spiroplot: The Files" later in this chapter). In the unlikely event that your PC has a character-mode-only display, Spiroplot will not work on your system. Spiroplot is smart enough to recognize this and will give you an error message.

Escaping Spiroplot

Escaping Spiroplot is a two-step maneuver: pressing <Esc> while running a demo or entering values will return you to the main menu; at this point, pressing **Q** (or moving the cursor to the immediate right of the Quit command) will cause the program to inquire: "Ok to quite Spiroplot? (Y/N)." Pressing **N** will keep the program running; pressing **Y** (or any other key, except N) will end the program.

Note: we do not recommend using <Ctrl>-<Break> as a method of exiting Spiroplot. While the command does produce an exit from the program, it leaves some displays (most notably CGA) in an unusable state thereafter, forcing you to reboot in order to resume computing. The built-in exit works and restores the display to a workable state; we recommend you use that technique instead.

Suggestions for Using Spiroplot

We recommend using Spiroplot first and foremost as a fun, fascinating, fabulous way to waste time and make your own pretty pictures on the screen. As we mentioned earlier, running the SPIRO.DEM demonstration file also makes a nice screen blanker. If any kids have access to the machine, let them get a chance to play with it—then you'll get a feel for what this program can do.

Spiroplot: The Fine Print

Spiroplot 2.0 Copyright © Donald MacFarlane 1990. The program is free and can be freely distributed as long as no fee is charged for the program, and the program and the documentation are distributed in their original, unmodified state. The graphic driver files (*.BGI) that accompany the program are proprietary to Borland International (the maker of the Pascal compiler used to build the program) and must not be given or used apart from their association with the Spiroplot program.

Mr. MacFarlane requests feedback from users and will also supply the source code for the program for a fee ($12.00 for 5.25" disks, $13.00 for 3.5" disks; checks or money orders in U.S. dollars are requested). He also asks that if you come up with any particularly dazzling plots, that you share the parameters with him for inclusion in SPIRO.DEM. You can contact him at 80 Browning Ave., Nashua, NH 03062. On CompuServe, his ID is 72411,2146.

Spiroplot: The Files

The following files make up the Spiroplot environment:

.BGI files	Borland Turbo Pascal graphics drivers
ATT.BGI	Device driver for AT&T 6300
CGA.BGI	Device driver for CGA and MCGA
EGAVGA.BGI	Device driver for EGA and VGA
HERC.BGI	Device driver for Hercules mono

PC3270.BGI	Device driver for PC3270
IBM8514.BGI	Device driver for IBM 8514 card
SPIRO.DEM	Spiroplot demonstration file
SPIRO.DOC	Spiroplot user guide (worth reading); lots of additional details on the program
SPIRO.EXE	Spiroplot program

BUGRES

 "Amusing insects to eat your screen"

What BUGRES Does

BUGRES is a TSR that is activated by a simple key combination (<Alt>-B), with some pretty amusing results. As TSRs go, it's quite small (0.3 KB of environment and 9.8 KB of program, for a total of about 11,000 bytes), yet it provides one of the most entertaining screen blankers we've encountered. For your own amusement, it's fun to watch BUGRES do its thing; for the unsuspecting, it can be a horrifying sight to watch little goblins systematically devour the contents of the screen. The program is entirely character based, and the bugs seem mostly to be composed of O's and right and left slashes. Figure 17, *BUGRES Creatures*, shows a simulated rogue's gallery of these dastardly creatures.

There are also diagonal critters that are variations on the same theme (but a little harder to capture for analysis, as we did in Figure 17).

BUGRES is benign; it saves the contents of the screen before it starts munching, and all it takes to stop the attack is a single keystroke, of any key. However, the visual effects are interesting, and the reactions of the unsuspecting are often worth watching.

```
    0           \ /         \ \          / /

   / \          \ /          0            0

   / \           0          / /          \ \
  _____

    A            B            C            D
```

Figure 17. BUGRES Creatures:
The four different "bugs" in BUGRES. Types A and B are upward and downward moving, respectively; Types C and D are rightward and lcftward moving, respectively.

How to Use BUGRES

Using BUGRES couldn't be simpler: It accepts no parameters and requires no switches or any other additional values. It is invoked by entering the name of the program, BUGRES, at the DOS prompt. Assuming that you've used our directory structure for SPCTs, you'd enter the following string:

C:\\>C:\\STUP-PC\\BUGRES\\BUGRES

As TSRs go, BUGRES is reasonably intelligent. It recognizes when it's already been loaded and will not permit multiple copies of itself to be installed at the same time. Whenever you want to activate BUGRES, enter <Ctrl>-B; to deactivate BUGRES, press any key (this behavior makes it impossible to capture a screen shot of the program at work, however, and that's why we can't furnish you with anything but a few crude illustrations, as depicted in Figure 17).

Warning: When this program is loaded and run with EXPLOSIV, your cursor will disappear when you exit EXPLOSIV with the <Esc> key. We recommend running one or the other, not both.

Escaping BUGRES

All it takes to stop a BUGRES attack is a single keystroke, but because it's a TSR, BUGRES hangs around after it's installed. It can be removed by rebooting your machine with <Ctrl>-<Alt>-<Del>), or by using a TSR management tool to remove it explicitly (for more information, see Appendix A, "Managing TSRs").

Suggestions for Using BUGRES

BUGRES is a screen blanker: It occupies your DOS display while you're not using your machine to keep the entire screen active, thereby avoiding the inevitable burn-out of particular portions of the display over time (for instance, a very large number of DOS displays have a C:\> prompt permanently etched into the upper lefthand corner of the display). Once installed, BUGRES can be invoked at any time by entering <Ctrl>-B at the keyboard. We recommend that you get in the habit of doing this any time you leave your machine unattended (or when you break off using it to do other things) for more than a few minutes at a stretch.

BUGRES: The Fine Print

BUGRES is freeware, the work of SSgt. Kenneth Leesman, of Omaha, Nebraska. SSgt. Leesman is a member of the Air Force and spends a great deal of his spare time happily hacking away at his computer. BUGRES is only one of the many fine programs he's written, and we hope to see more made available to the public soon.

BUGRES Files

There's only one file in the BUGRES program, and it includes all the instructions about running the program that you'll need:

BUGRES.COM   Program file, with operating
                              instructions

SAYINGS

 "Words of wisdom for any occasion"

What SAYINGS Does

SAYINGS displays a "thought for the day" in a window on the PC's screen, until any key is pressed (at which point the window and its message disappear). SAYINGS draws its material from an easily edited ASCII text file called SAYINGS.DAT that can reside anywhere in your DOS PATH. Figure 18, *You Don't Say-ings*, shows a couple of SAYINGS's sayings. By and large, these illustrations also show what the program displays and the types of sayings that the program includes.

SAYINGS uses a random number generator to select one of the lines in the SAYINGS.DAT file to supply its words of wisdom whenever it's called. To avoid repetition, or to ensure a customized sayings environment, we recommend that you edit the SAYINGS.DAT file, to add more material and to customize what's already there.

How to Use SAYINGS

SAYINGS can be included in .BAT files or accessed directly at the DOS prompt. For instance, including the following line in your AUTOEXEC.BAT file will get you a saying every time you start your computer up:

CD C:\STUP-PC\SAYINGS

SAYINGS

We recommend putting it in as the last line, so you'll remember to clear the screen by pressing a key.

SAYINGS can be called on to provide its ineffable wisdom any time you want, simply by entering the same string at any time at the DOS prompt.

Escaping SAYINGS

Since it's a program (not a TSR), no special cleanup is necessary: Once you're finished with it, it's finished with you!

Editing SAYINGS.DAT

One of SAYINGS's interesting qualities is that it automatically sizes the window in which it displays the currently selected saying by counting the number of characters in each individual line segment in the saying that it has selected to display. The end of each message is indicated by the carriage return at the end of each line in the text file. In English, this means that you have to be able to fit each saying onto a single line of text within the SAYINGS.DAT file, or you'll wind up with partial messages.

To break a saying as it occurs in the SAYINGS.DAT file into multiple lines when displayed, use the vertical slash character (|) as a separator in the text. For example, entering the string "Roses are red, | Violets are blue, | DOS is my buddy, | I'm not sure about you!" on a single line into the SAYINGS.DAT file would result in the following output (within a windowed border when displayed):

94

Roses are red,

Violets are blue,

DOS is my buddy,

I'm not sure about you!

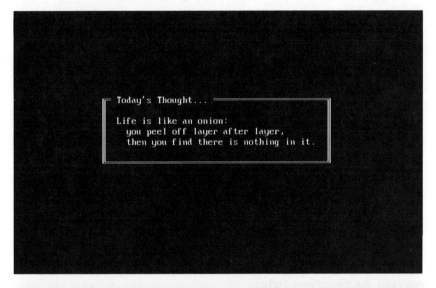

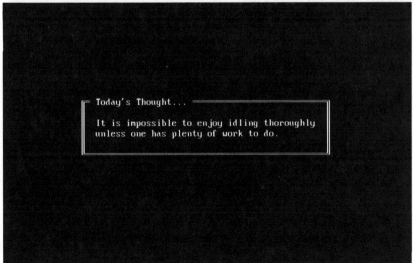

Figure 18. You Don't Say-ings:
Two of SAYINGS's included messages.

To get a blank line, insert two vertical slashes (| |) next to each other; for two or more blank lines, one vertical slash more than the number of blank lines desired will do the trick (for example, to get four blank lines, use five vertical slashes).

To edit SAYINGS.DAT, use the built-in DOS editor, EDLIN, or any other editor that can handle text only (ASCII) files. If you use a word processor, be sure to save the file as text only, sometimes called "pure ASCII."

Suggestions for Using SAYINGS

SAYINGS makes a diverting addition to one's own local environment, so we recommend installing it in your AUTOEXEC.BAT file and invoking it whenever you want a word or two of wisdom. You can also install it as a trick, but this one is enough of a treat not to warrant retaliatory action. You can also make SAYINGS available to network users, where use of a network-wide path or drive mapping will point everybody at SAYINGS.DAT and access to the SAYINGS.EXE program will permit them to share it freely.

SAYINGS: The Fine Print

SAYINGS is a freeware program written by Scott Wertz (we couldn't obtain an address for Mr. Wertz, but his CompuServe ID is 71541,3051). Feel free to share SAYINGS with your colleagues and co-workers, and don't forget that editing the SAYINGS.DAT file makes it even more fun to use (and to inflict on others).

SAYINGS: The Files

The files included with the SAYINGS program include:

SAYINGS.DAT	Text file containing sayings to be displayed
SAYINGS.EXE	SAYINGS program
SAYREAD.DOC	Brief program documentation file (worth reading)

WILLTE

 "The Lone Ranger rides again!"

What WILLTE Does

WILLTE is an electronic transcription of Gioachino Rossini's immortal "William Tell Overture," known to culture buffs and fans of Tonto and the Lone Ranger everywhere. Even in this book, it's a nonpareil of an SPCT, since all it can do is play the song.

How to Use WILLTE

You invoke WILLTE by entering the name of the program. As long as the program is somewhere on the user's DOS PATH, the Masked Man will ride again! (For more information on the DOS PATH, see the glossary at the end of the book.) Also, you can run it from anywhere by typing **C:\STUP-PC\WILLTE\WILLTE**.

Escaping WILLTE

WILLTE is a program, not a TSR, so when it's over, it's out of the DOS environment. However, the screen that displays itself while the "William Tell Overture" is in action isn't kidding: It really does take 3 minutes, 12 seconds for this thing to play itself all the way to its thrilling conclusion (see Figure 19, *3 Minutes, 12 Seconds* for a picture of what could get to be an overly familiar screen to its unwilling victims).

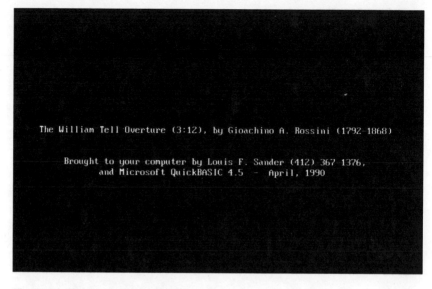

The William Tell Overture (3:12), by Gioachino A. Rossini (1792-1868)

Brought to your computer by Louis F. Sander (412) 367-1376,
and Microsoft QuickBASIC 4.5 - April, 1990

Figure 19. 3 Minutes, 12 Seconds:
You'll see this screen the whole time the overture is playing.

For those who know the song already, or who don't want to wait while the song builds to its climactic conclusion, there is a trick for bailing out. By simultaneously pressing <Ctrl>-<Break> (or <Scroll Lock> on some keyboards), WILLTE can be forced to cease and desist. Most DOS programs respond to this kind of termination as well as the more common <Ctrl>-C, but those who don't know this bailout will either have to reboot or wait for the song to play its seemingly interminable way to completion!

Suggestions for Using WILLTE

The same batch file technique outlined in the chapter on BUGLE works very well if you want to slip the "William Tell Overture" over on the unsuspecting. By renaming a program and substituting a batch file that calls WILLTE before calling the program, it can be made into an integral part of using the program—at least as far as the victim is concerned.

98

WILLTE: The Fine Print

WILLTE is brought to you by the same man who brought you BUGLE—Louis F. Sander. This program is freeware and may be shared with your friends and co-workers. Who knows, it could cause a renaissance of the late, lamented Lone Ranger cult!

WILLTE: The Files

WILLTE consists of a single file:

> WILLTE.EXE   Plays the "William Tell Overture"

ANNOY

 "The PC turns on its master!"

What ANNOY Does

ANNOY is advertised by its author as "The irritating DOS shell," and this is clearly one product that lives up to its claims. It's also clearly intended to permit you to do unto others before they can do likewise unto you, so proceed with caution.

ANNOY is a miniature DOS shell. It accepts (or rather intercepts) all DOS input and executes it as entered. However, if a particular command has been set up to be annoying (in the spirit of the program), ANNOY will first sound an alarm and then will require the unsuspecting user to enter a password before allowing him or her to continue with whatever work is at hand.

The password request is intended as an annoyance, because any response will do. The annoyance it provides stems from its association to commonly or frequently used DOS commands (such as CD, DIR, and so on) that require the user to jump through a hoop every time he or she wants to use it before getting on with business. Figure 20, *Password Annoyance*, depicts ANNOY's response to a keyword when it's entered.

```
What ! You want to 'test' *AGAIN*?
If you keep using 'test', you're going to WEAR IT OUT!
Enter the secret, magical password, and the mystical powers
within this omniscient computer may allow entry
into 'test'
(If you don't know the password, just guess. The computer might not EXPLODE.)
?

LUCKY GUESS!
C:\>
```

Figure 20. Password Annoyance:
ANNOY forces you to type in a password before executing the specified command (test, in this example).

But wait—there's more! Should the user enter obscenities at the
keyboard, ANNOY will recognize some common ones (of the four-
letter-word variety, anyway) and will recommend use of the DOS
HELP command instead. The beauty of this recommendation is that
HELP is always set up to require the annoying password, thereby
compounding the aggravation.

How to Use ANNOY

As a shell replacement, ANNOY is more than just a TSR. Because it
is the first stop-off point for all keyboard input, it is actually running
the (victim's) PC most of the time. It is invoked with a password,
followed by a list of keywords to trigger the ANNOY response (the
syntax for the command is as follows):

C:\STUP-PC\ANNOY>**ANNOY** **<password>** **<kw1>**
<kw2>...<kwn>

The following table explains the commands:

Command	Explanation
Password	Can be any ASCII string. It turns ANNOY off if correctly entered. It must be entered as a DOS command in order to take effect.
kw1...n	The keywords intended to trigger the ANNOY response. Ideally, these should be common DOS commands or the names of frequently used programs (e.g., 123, WP, and so on). Separate keywords by blanks (up to about 100 characters' worth of names, including blanks, can be used, so you can really go wild).

Escaping ANNOY

As a DOS command shell replacement, ANNOY is rather large: It requires about 77 KB of memory. (Actually, about 65 KB of this is required for DOS, so it really only adds about 12 KB of additional overhead to your operating environment.)

Since it takes over for DOS, this means that you should absolutely *never* put ANNOY into co-workers' AUTOEXEC.BAT files unless you're prepared to help bail them out, or you know that they understand DOS well enough to figure it out for themselves. While a certain amount of trickery with the SPCTs is inevitable, getting victims into more trouble than they can handle is irresponsible, unless you're willing to lend a hand to get things back to normal.

To escape from ANNOY's irritating influence, you have to reboot your PC (use the three-fingered salute, <Ctrl>-<Alt>-<Del>). Another option is to use a TSR management tool to remove ANNOY from your environment. (See Appendix A, "Managing TSRs," for detailed information about TSR management tools.)

Suggestions for Using ANNOY

The program's author recommends setting up ANNOY on your own machine as a means of frustrating uninvited interlopers who use your machine while you're absent. We also recognize that ANNOY has obvious appeal (and limitless applications) as a means of harassing colleagues and co-workers, so all we can do is egg you on but also recommend that you be both mischievous and responsible.

ANNOY: The Fine Print

ANNOY is the product of Matthew Ratcliff, an Electrical Engineer and confessed "compute-a-holic" with a five-compile a day habit. ANNOY is a shareware program, for which a $5.00 donation is requested (we think that it's worth the money, as SPCTs go). Send your contributions to Ratware Softworks, 32 South Hartnett Ave., St. Louis, MO 63135.

ANNOY: The Files

ANNOY's files include the following:

ANNOY.C	C language source code for ANNOY program
ANNOY.DOC	ANNOY documentation file (worth reading)
ANNOY.EXE	ANNOY program

ANNOY can also create a log file to keep track of activities that trigger the ANNOY response if the user elects to supply a name for the log. We tended to use the filename ANNOY.LOG so we'd know what to make of the filename later on.

RREALM

 "The mysterious world of fractal geometry"

What RREALM Does

RREALM stands for Recursive Realm. It is a toolkit for playing with fractals, a branch of mathematics named by Benoit Mandelbrot, after whom the basic fractal function, the Mandelbrot Set, is named.

Lest it sound totally dry and boring (as too many people think is the case with mathematics), we hasten to add that the primary tool for fractal study appears to be generating and viewing stunning color images. RREALM is primarily a tool for creating and viewing such images, and it's a pleasure to work with.

Fractal geometry is not a stupid topic, whether implemented for DOS or otherwise. However, some of our criteria for selecting programs for this book were that candidate programs be time-consuming, addictive, or have little or no socially redeeming value in addition to being as mindless as possible. In this case, it passed the first three tests with such flying colors that the last one had to be overlooked.

One of the most interesting aspects of fractal images is that they are recursive in nature (hence the name of this program). What this means is that any view of a fractal contains all other views, provided that you zoom in enough (or out enough) to appreciate this phenomenon. The start-up activities in RREALM consist of selecting and tuning a fractal function and creating an initial display; after these preliminaries, one can literally spend days zooming in on various regions of the plots for further investigation.

Special RREALM Requirements

Now that we've gotten you excited about this wonderful program, there's one sad note to the story: RREALM will only work with an EGA or VGA color monitor. It also requires at least 256 KB of available RAM.

Because of the intense computational requirements of RREALM's images, a math co-processor will greatly speed up the process (we noticed a 150 to 250 percent performance improvement in otherwise identical environments, with and without a math co-processor). The CONFIG.SYS file must include the ANSI.SYS file. See your DOS manual for details; this generally requires that a line reading

DEVICE = ANSI.SYS

be included in your CONFIG.SYS file.

How to Use RREALM

RREALM is entirely menu-driven, so it's easy to explore. Figure 21, *RREALM Startup,* depicts the start-up menu, showing the types of choices that users have when entering the program.

The basic activities center around exploring the types of mathematical functions that RREALM supports. These include the Mandelbrot set, the granddaddy of all fractal mathematics; the Julia set, an exploration of Newton's Method; and a model to simulate magnetic fields that the author calls "Phases for Magnetism."

Once a particular function family is selected, the user selects values for the function and a view of how that function is to be displayed. Because the color plots that RREALM produces are complex and colorful, this is a good activity to fire off before going to bed one night so that you can view the results the next morning (this is especially true if you don't have a math co-processor to speed

Figure 21. RREALM Startup:
When you start RREALM, you can choose from several activities.

up the calculations that go into drawing the pictures). Figure 22, *Newton's Choices*, shows the set of choices for Newton's Method, including function specification and window size.

Once a particular image is generated, you can select a view into that image to zoom in on regions of particular interest. Since these functions are recursive, each one supports as much detail as the graphics display equipment on the computer can provide (the functions themselves iterate happily onto infinity). This characteristic permits detailed investigation of any image and provides one of the most fascinating ways to consume large amounts of CPU time that we've ever encountered. A sample image is shown in Figure 23, *MandelShot*. This black-and-white recreation doesn't do justice to the beauty of these images on a color monitor, however.

Once a collection of images has been established, RREALM allows them to be "animated"—that is, displayed in sequence, as an ever-shifting panoply of images. A good way to get a feel for the program is to animate the images that are supplied with it. This by itself was more than enough to get us hooked on the program, and it has provided many hours of entertainment since then.

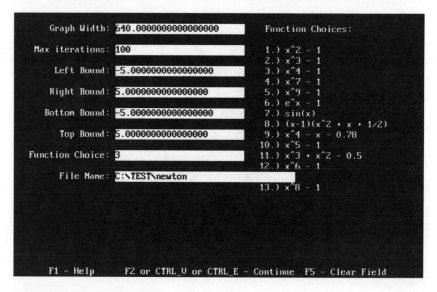

```
    Graph Width: 640.0000000000000000        Function Choices:

 Max iterations: 100                         1.) x^2 - 1
                                             2.) x^3 - 1
    Left Bound: -5.0000000000000000          3.) x^4 - 1
                                             4.) x^7 - 1
   Right Bound: 5.0000000000000000           5.) x^9 - 1
                                             6.) e^x - 1
  Bottom Bound: -5.0000000000000000          7.) sin(x)
                                             8.) (x-1)(x^2 + x + 1/2)
    Top Bound: 5.0000000000000000            9.) x^4 - x - 0.78
                                             10.) x^5 - 1
Function Choice: 8                           11.) x^3 + x^2 - 0.5
                                             12.) x^6 - 1
    File Name: C:\TEST\newton
                                             13.) x^8 - 1




 F1 - Help        F2 or CTRL_U or CTRL_E - Continue  F5 - Clear Field
```

Figure 22. Newton's Choices:
Choices for generating an image using Newton's Method.

Figure 23. MandelShot:
This black-and-white screen shot doesn't begin to do justice to the beautiful
color images that RREALM can create.

108

Escaping RREALM

The author has taken complete control over the keyboard in RREALM: The only ways to exit (short of the three-fingered salute) are those that the program itself explicitly provides. At any point, <Esc> returns you to the main menu screen, whereupon entering <Esc> again, you will trigger the inquiry "Exit to DOS? (Y/N)." This inquiry only responds to the Y and N keys (and no others) with the expected behavior: Entering **Y** ends the program and displays an exit screen with registration and other program information; **N** returns you to the main menu.

Suggestions for Using RREALM

We don't have enough space to do anything approaching justice to this program in the book, but the author was kind enough to include an exhaustive and instructive user guide (RREALM.DOC) as a part of the overall package. We strongly recommend that you print this manual and read through it before getting serious about working with RREALM.

You can press <F1> at any time within the program to get useful, on-screen help. Pages 11 and 12 of the user guide provide a quick look at RREALM, pages 13–28 provide all of the gory program details, and pages 29–36 feature appendices that explain how to get the best use of the program, including an exhaustive bibliography for further reading on the subject. Rather than repeating this information, we prefer to point you in the right direction. Enjoy!

RREALM: The Fine Print

RREALM is a shareware product by Scott Jones. You can freely copy and share RREALM with others, as long as you don't charge for the program, you don't modify it, and you distribute it with all of its support files intact.

You are granted a license to try RREALM for a period of 30 days. If you continue to use it after that time, please register by sending a $20.00 registration fee (checks or money orders only; CA residents add 6.5 percent sales tax) to its author, Scott Jones, at Route 3, 22514 West Gibson, Buckeye, AZ 85326.

The registration fee entitles you to use this software on a single computer and to make as many copies as you wish for backup purposes or for distribution. When you register, you will be issued a registration number and instructions on how to integrate it with your copy of the software.

Registration confers some additional benefits: The program will be personalized with your name, and the shareware screen that is normally displayed when you exit the program will be suppressed. Registered users will also receive the latest version of the RREALM program, a 360 KB floppy with some new and interesting images, and will be notified whenever new versions become available. Please check the documentation file, RREALM.DOC, for a registration form. You can find it on page 37, the final page of that file.

RREALM: The Files

RREALM is the largest program in our SPCT collection, and it includes the greatest number of files. We list some of them by extension only, rather than in detail, but all relevant extensions are included:

RR.EXE	Recursive Realm program
Picture Files	Picture and data files for image display
*.RRM	Mandelbrot set picture files
*.RRJ	Julia set picture files
*.RRN	Newton's Method picture files
*.RRP	Magnetism picture files (none supplied)
*.DAT	Data files to drive various functions
RRWELC.OME	Recursive Realm welcome screen

RREALM.DOC	User guide (37 pages; well worth reading)
RRPICS.CAT	Recursive Realm picture catalog

The only conflict with the picture file extension is the data file for the SAYINGS program, which is named SAYINGS.DAT. All other files ending with a .DAT extension belong to RREALM.

Appendix A: Managing TSRs

TSR Basics

DOS was built around Intel's family of 80X86 family of microprocessors. From the earliest 8086-based IBM PC to the current 80386- and 80486-based machines, all of these microprocessors are related and share a common ability to provide a hospitable environment for the DOS operating system (even if this means that only a fraction of their capability is being used, as is the case with the newer, more powerful 80386 and 80486 versions).

Terminate-and-stay-resident (TSR) programs were originally introduced by Microsoft as a way of providing print services on a PC. The earliest TSR was written to permit a PC to communicate with a printer in the background while permitting the PC to respond to input from the keyboard. A number of clever programmers reverse-engineered the mechanism built into the PRINT command and used a similar approach in writing programs that came to be known as TSRs.

The Pros and Cons of TSRs

TSRs have several advantages. Because they remain installed in memory even when they're not being used, they're never more than a set of keystrokes away from whatever you're doing, no matter what program you may be running. For this reason, TSRs are very popular for address and phone books, notepads, calculators, and other basic desktop utilities. Since phone calls and other types of interruptions that may require access to certain information can occur at any time, it's convenient to be able to access such things at any time while using your computer.

A need for constant or rapid access is also what makes TSRs attractive for device drivers, which are programs that are used to permit computers to communicate with specific peripherals or other specialized hardware components. Although Microsoft's PRINT driver originally launched the TSR phenomenon, TSRs are equally important for network access, scanning devices, facsimile capabilities, and other specialized functions.

The positive aspect of TSRs can be summed up in three ways: convenience, speed, and extension of basic functionality. Both utility TSRs and device drivers partake of all three qualities and have proven themselves invaluable in permitting users to customize their working environments.

If TSRs have such great capabilities, what are the negative aspects? The DOS environment has a limited amount of random-access memory (RAM) that it can work with directly. Even though newer 80X86 microprocessors can support large amounts of RAM (from 16 MB to as much as 4 gigabytes), none of this is directly accessible to DOS.

The amount of RAM that is directly accessible is limited by the architecture of the earliest members of the family to a maximum of 1 MB (1024 KB), broken into two chunks: a 640 KB section directly available for program and operating system use under DOS and another 384 KB set aside for reserved device use for working space (buffers) and for speeding up the performance of information originally stored in read-only memory (ROM) on the earliest 8086 and 8088 Intel microprocessors. Figure 24, *DOS RAM Map,* shows how this memory is addressed.

Memory Region	Decimal	Segment	
	0 KB	0	
	64 KB	1000	
	128 KB	2000	
	192 KB	3000	
640 KB DOS Program Area	256 KB	4000	
	320 KB	5000	
	384 KB	6000	
	448 KB	7000	
	512 KB	8000	
	576 KB	9000	
384 KB Reserved Area	640 KB	A000	EGA Displays
	704 KB	B000	Video (incl. EGA)
	768 KB	C000	EGA ROM, Bernouilli
	832 KB	D000	ARCNET, Token-Ring, EMS
	896 KB	E000	PC/AT Reserved ROM Space
	960 KB	F000	ROM BIOS
Extended/ Expanded RAM	1 MB- 16 MB		

Figure 24. DOS RAM Map:
1. DOS memory is arranged in 64 KB segments (640 KB area is 10 segments, 384 KB area is 6 segments).
2. Reserved area is used for device drivers (video, tape drive, and network interface cards) and for reserved ROM and ROM BIOS mapping.
3. Area above 1 MB is available in protected mode to 80286 and higher; mapping area for EMS memory systems (map to D000 segment).

All this explanation has been needed for the following claim to be intelligible: The primary limitation of TSRs results from their "stay-resident" characteristic. Because the amount of RAM that is available to DOS is fixed, and because programs are getting larger all the time, giving up space to accommodate TSRs is becoming more problematical as time goes by.

Dealing with the DOS RAM Ceiling

The phenomenon of trying to squeeze more functionality into a limited space is called "RAM cram" and has led to several interesting tricks with DOS memory since 1985. All these efforts have resulted from the continued (and increasing) popularity of DOS as a desktop environment coupled with profound pressure to realize more computing capability on those desktops.

TSRs are always subject to more refined and subtle programming tricks to make them as small as possible. There are several approaches to expanding the scope of DOS memory that can permit TSRs to be moved out of the 640 KB space reserved for DOS, either into the 384 KB region originally designed for device support, or into the regions above 1 MB, where only the 80286, 80386, and 80486 microprocessors can get to directly.

How TSRs Behave

Understanding how TSRs work is easy with the use of a few diagrams. Using the framework for DOS memory depicted in Figure 24, we can show how TSRs operate in a normal, unaugmented DOS environment (where relocation to the reserved 384 KB region or to areas above 1 MB is not used or is not available). This is depicted in Figures 25, *DOS + TSR,* and 26, *DOS + TSR A + TSR B,* where two TSRs, named TSR A and TSR B, respectively, are added to the environment.

In examining Figures 25 and 26, please note that we lose a portion of the 640 KB available to programs just by running DOS (it usually requires around 65 KB or so) and that TSRs are added on top of DOS in the order in which they are installed. Whatever space in the 640 KB area is left over after DOS and the TSRs are in place is all that's available for use by programs.

When a PC gets rebooted, all programs get flushed from memory. This includes DOS, all TSRs, and whatever else—typically some application—may be running at the time. DOS is automatically reinstalled when the computer starts running, because it provides the environment that permits your PC to operate (without DOS or some other operating system, a PC is basically an expensive, oversized paperweight).

116

Memory Region	Decimal	Segment	Explanation

	0 KB	0	Memory Area Size Description 0000-003F 1 K Interrupt area 0040-004F 0.3 K BIOS data area
	64 KB	1000	0050-006F 0.5 K System data 0070-0E8C 56 K DOS 0E8D-10F4 9.6 K TSR A
	128 KB	2000	10F5-9FFF 572 [Available]
DOS Program Area 640 KB	192 KB	3000	
	256 KB	4000	
	320 KB	5000	
	384 KB	6000	
	448 KB	7000	
	512 KB	8000	
	576 KB	9000	

Figure 25. DOS + TSR A:
1. TSR A is added right after DOS, beginning with address 0E8D up through 10F4.
2. The available program area is decremented by the size of TSR A (9.6 KB).

Memory Region	Decimal	Segment	Explanation

	0 KB	0	Memory Area Size Description 0000-003F 1 K Interrupt area 0040-004F 0.3 K BIOS data area
	64 KB	1000	0050-006F 0.5 K System data 0070-0E8C 56 K DOS 0E8D-10F4 9.6 K TSR A
	128 KB	2000	10F5-1AF4 10 TSR B 1AF5-9FFF K [Available]
DOS Program Area 640 KB	192 KB	3000	
	256 KB	4000	
	320 KB	5000	
	384 KB	6000	
	448 KB	7000	
	512 KB	8000	
	576 KB	9000	

Figure 26. DOS + TSR A + TSR B:
1. TSR A is added right after DOS, beginning with address 0E8D up through 10F4.
2. TSR B follows TSR A, starting at 10F5 through 1AF4.
3. The available program area is decremented by the size of TSR B (10 KB).

117

Device driver TSRs are typically installed by the CONFIG.SYS file and utility TSRs by the AUTOEXEC.BAT file. When troubleshooting conflicts or mysterious problems arise, you should check both files and subject them to a process of elimination, if necessary, to catch any potential troublemakers. Manually installed TSRs simply fail to reappear when a machine is rebooted, largely because they are no longer installed. This is why rebooting the PC works so well to get rid of the SPCTs that are also TSRs.

The order of installation is important, because it affects the procedure needed to remove TSRs once they are in place. There are a number of tools that can control TSRs, including installation and removal, without rebooting being necessary. In most cases, managing TSRs behaves like a stack (or an onion, in more prosaic terms). TSRs must be installed from the bottom up and removed from the top down.

If you had three TSRs installed in the order A-B-C and you wanted to remove C, it would be easy: All you would have to do is instruct your TSR management tool (see the next section) to remove C and be done with it. Removing elements in the middle of the stack is a two-step operation: First, you have to remove all TSRs from the top down to get to the one you actually want to remove; and second, you have to to reinstall the ones that are above the one you want to remove. Thus to remove A, the sequence would be as follows: remove C, remove B, remove A, install B, install C (see Figure 27, *Removing and Reinstalling TSRs*).

As long as you remember the basic rules of how TSRs are installed, working with them is fairly easy.

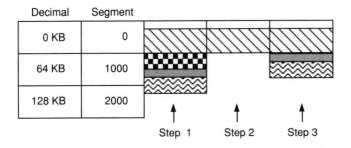

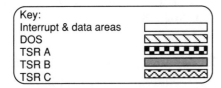

Figure 27. Removing and Reinstalling TSRs:
Step 1: TSRs A, B, and C are installed. The goal is to remove A.
Step 2: All TSRs from the base of free memory through and including A are removed.
Step 3: TSRs B and C are re-installed. The net effect is the removal of A and the preservation of B and C.

Some TSR Tools

Because TSRs are so popular (some might even say ubiquitous), there is a wide variety of tools available for their management. Our highest recommendation goes to a collection of shareware utilities for TSR management called TSR Utilities by its author, Kim Kokkenen.

This software is available from a variety of bulletin boards, preferably CompuServe (BPROGA forum, LIB 2), or for a modest registration fee ($20.00) directly from the author. Send checks or money orders to: TurboPower Software, P.O. Box 66747, Scotts Valley, CA 95066-0747. Questions can also be sent via electronic mail to TurboPower Software's CompuServe ID: 72457,2131.

The TurboPower TSR Utilities provide tools that mark TSRs as they're being installed and that delete one or more of them based on their marks (and, of course, on their order of installation). These utilities also include a nifty set of tools for managing the NetWare shell for those of you who are running on a Novell network.

119

There is a broad selection of commercial TSR management utilities available in the marketplace, but we have had good results with the following packages (most of which offer comprehensive memory management environments, far more than simple TSR management).

Product:	386MAX
Company:	Qualitas, Inc. 7101 Wisconsin Ave., Suite 1386 Bethesda, MD 20814 (301) 907-6700
Remarks:	Includes the ability to control and manage TSRs and loadability into extended or expanded RAM.
Products:	DESQView 386, DESQView, QRAM
Company:	Quarterdeck Office Systems 150 Pico Blvd. Santa Monica, CA 90405 (213) 392-9701
Remarks:	DESQview is a multitasking, window-oriented DOS environment for 386 or 286 processors that does a lot more than manage memory. QRAM is a 286-specific memory manager that offers good TSR control. All these programs include an excellent memory mapping and management utility called Manifest.
Product:	RAM Lord
Company:	Waterworks Software, Inc. 913 Electric Ave. Seal Beach, CA 90740 (213) 594-4768

Remarks: Permits sets of TSRs to be defined and
                 swapped to and from disk as needed (good
                 TSR management system).

Each of these products has its strengths and weaknesses, and
some are far more powerful than others. However, all of them
support the ability to map memory and to install and remove TSRs
at will.

Relocating TSRs

Relocating a TSR means running it in some location outside the
normal 640 KB of DOS program space. Doing so requires the use of
a memory manager, such as 386MAX or DESQview, to manage
relocating the TSR, either to the 384 KB reserved area or to an
address over 1 MB. The memory manager will also handle commu-
nications from the PC to the TSR as its agent. Since most TSRs are
activated by specific keystrokes, this means that the memory manager makes sure that the TSR behaves as expected, even if it is
running in an unusual memory location.

Even when as much of DOS itself and all the device drivers and
TSRs are relocated, it's rare that this will free up more than 600 KB
of DOS program space (we've observed some installations with as
much as 620 KB, but this takes lots of fine-tuning and experimen-
tation to make optimal). There are certain parts of DOS that cannot
be relocated, and the memory manager must maintain a portion of
itself in the 640 KB space to intercept TSR-bound keystrokes and
messages in order to support normal operation.

The benefits of this kind of setup are meaningful to those for whom
application space is vital. This may not be as small a group as one
might think, because there is a growing number of large applications, such as AutoCAD, Ventura Publisher, and MicroGraphix
Designer, all of which require at least 550 KB of free RAM with which
to work. The costs of adding memory and the software to control it
are often outweighed by the convenience and familiarity of being
able to maintain a stable of TSRs. We strongly recommend further
investigation for PC users who have such needs.

121

Appendix B:
Building
Floppies

General Information

You can order floppies from us, if you need different sizes from those included with this book. If so, see the order form at the end of the book. This appendix teaches you how to build floppies so you don't have to order them from us. Doing so will require access to a machine with a hard disk with about 2.5 MB of free space and the right kind of floppy drive to create the desired type of decompressed floppies for actual use. The number of floppies that result will depend on the size and kind of floppy used: for the highest capacity, this will be one or two floppies (3.5" HD, 1.44 MB); for the lowest capacity in common use, this will be four or five floppies (5.25", 360 KB).

Floppy Setup

We strongly recommend that you FORMAT the floppies for use with the tricks with the /S parameter, to make the floppies bootable (this will prevent unnecessary disk swapping later on). This process requires about 70 KB of disk space per floppy and may require the higher of the two numbers of floppies indicated in the previous

123

section. (Note: If you have need of special files like CONFIG.SYS or AUTOEXEC.BAT in order to run some of the SPCTs, you'll have to copy these files over as well. Please check the requirements for each trick you want on the disk.)

Floppy Copies

Once the floppies are formatted, they're ready to receive the decompressed SPCT files. The guiding concept is to group all the pieces for an individual trick together on the same floppy so that all requisite information will be together when you need it.

To begin the process, proceed as the book directs: Copy the contents of the original floppy onto the transfer computer's hard disk and decompress the files. We recommend running the STUPID.BAT program to organize the tricks files, but that is a matter of personal choice. If you do not elect to run the batch file, read the Files section at the end of each chapter to make sure you copy all relevant files for a particular trick to a single floppy.

Selecting Floppy Contents

There are 17 tricks altogether, varying in size from about 5 KB to 515 KB . (The latter is RREALM and its associated files. It obviously will not fit onto a 360K floppy; however, its CPU demands make it unsuitable for a floppy-only machine, anyway.) Careful mixing and matching of the various tricks will let you compose the floppies that work best for you (or that fit best, at any rate).

Whenever you create a floppy, make sure to leave at least 20 KB of available space on it. This will leave room for temporary files, working space, and other applications or tricks, as you continue to fine-tune your environment.

Glossary

\<Alt\>

The way we denote the key labeled "Alt"on the DOS keyboard; in most DOS applications the \<Alt\> key is used to modify the meaning of other keys (it is used in combination with other keys). We use the angle brackets (\< \>) to enclose the names of specific keys so that you can easily recognize them as keys.

Application (a.k.a. Program)

Applications are programs that run when you enter their names at the DOS prompt. For example, to run the program ADULATE, enter its name as follows:

C:\>C:\STUP-PC\ADULATE\ADULATE.

Argument

Contrary to normal use, an argument in the DOS world refers to a value that is associated with a particular command. For instance, in the DOS command DIR *.BAT (which displays all batch files in the current default directory), *.BAT (the asterisk is a wildcard that can stand for any name) is an argument that tells DIR to display all files with any filename that has a .BAT extension.

ASCII

An abbreviation for American Standard Code for Information Interchange, pronounced ask-ee. ASCII assigns values ranging from 0 to 127 to characters of the alphabet, numbers, punctuation marks, and other special characters. Because these values are consistent on a majority of computers, ASCII character files can be easily exchanged between computers, even computers of different makes and models. ASCII files are also called text files.

AUTOEXEC.BAT

The file that is automatically executed whenever you start up your computer. It is used to install TSRs, establish the desired default directory, and establish a working environment whenever the computer is started or rebooted.

.BAT (or Batch File)

A file extension that indicates that the file contains a sequence of DOS commands. If a file named TEST.BAT is executed, for example, it will have the same results as if the commands it contained were entered, one after another, at the DOS keyboard. Batch files, as they are called, give even the most casual of DOS users a simple but useful programming capability. Batch files must be in plain text format, so remember to use an ASCII editor, not a word processor, to change them.

BIOS (Abbreviation for *Basic Input/Output System*)

A set of routines for accessing memory, disk, or other computer resources that is used by DOS to manage itself and the PC environment. BIOS routines are also available for use in programs that run in a DOS environment.

<Break>

The key on the DOS keyboard that is labeled "Break"; in most DOS applications the <Break> key is used to modify the meaning of other keys (it is used in combination with other keys). Sometimes the <Break> key is used to halt activity in certain programs. We use the angle brackets (< >) to enclose the names of specific keys so that you can easily recognize them as keys.

Byte

A byte is 8 bits (which may be either 0 or 1 in value) of data. It is a common basic unit for storage capacity (usually megabytes of disk space), speed (in bytes per second), and memory size (in kilobytes, especially for RAM).

CD

The DOS Change Directory command. It is used to change one's current default directory to another directory specification. For example, if your default directory is D:\TEST and you enter **CD D:\STUP-PC\ADULATE**, you will be located in the directory where the ADULATE program is placed by the STUPID.BAT program.

CGA (abbreviation for *Color Graphics Adapter*)

CGA is a fairly low resolution type of color display for a PC (usually rated at 640 horizontal by 200 vertical pixels). It was the earliest form of color display developed by IBM for the PC, and while it offered display of a maximum of 16 colors simultaneously, the resolution was so low that this option was seldom used. Likewise, CGA's text representation is crude and less readable than the more modern display types, such as EGA and VGA.

CLS

The DOS Clear Screen command. It instructs the PC to blank out the display and reset itself to its normal operating mode (very useful when bailing out of graphics or other programs).

CompuServe

An on-line information service, accessed using a modem, telecommunication software, and a telephone connection, that is available worldwide and contains a wealth of PC-related information and public domain software. It is also the leading meeting place for every conceivable variety of PC enthusiast. We found all the software in this book on CompuServe and recommend it as a source of information, inspiration, and diversion.

Controller

A controller is a special kind of PC adapter card that is typically used to manage access to a high-speed peripheral, such as a hard disk.

<Ctrl> or <Control>

The way we denote the specific DOS key labeled either as "Ctrl" or "Control"; in most DOS applications the Control key is used to modify the meaning of other keys (that is, it is used in combination with other keys). We use the angle brackets (< >) to enclose the names of specific keys so that you can easily recognize them as keys.

CPU (Abbreviation for *Central Processing Unit*)

The CPU is the brains of a computer. It contains the arithmetic and logical capacity that enables a computer to perform logical and mathematical computations, along with working space to permit values obtained from memory to be accessed and manipulated.

CRT (Abbreviation for *Cathode-Ray Tube*)

Any display device that uses a glass screen—for example, a TV set—is likely to be built around a CRT. The term is regularly used to describe a computer display, irrespective of graphics or color capability.

.DAT

A common DOS file extension that indicates that the file contains data of some kind, usually for the program whose filename coincides with that of the .DAT file (for example, it's a safe guess that SAYINGS.DAT contains data for the SAYINGS.EXE program).

Default Directory

In computer jargon, a default is what the computer assumes that you mean when you don't tell it exactly what to do. It is the preset condition. A default directory tells DOS the first place where you want it to look when you enter commands at the keyboard (the rest of the search hierarchy is supplied by the DOS PATH). The DOS design team decided that the default directory should be the one that you're currently in at any given time. Thus, the English equivalent for the term "default directory" is "the directory you're currently in."

<Del> or <Delete>

Denotes the specific DOS key labeled as either "Del" or "Delete" (in most applications, it deletes the character covered by the cursor). We use the angle brackets (< >) to enclose the names of specific keys so that you can easily recognize them as keys.

.DOC

A common file extension for documentation files in DOS file systems. For example, FOOL.DOC contains the documentation for the FOOL.EXE program.

DOS (Abbreviation for *Disk Operating System*)

DOS is the basic program that permits a PC to operate; it runs all the time and establishes the operating environment (also known as the operating system). The earliest PC versions ran from a floppy disk only; hence the name Disk Operating System.

DOS Command Interpreter

The command interpreter is that part of DOS that is responsible for reading what's being entered at the keyboard. It recognizes valid commands and passes them on to the correct DOS program so that they can be executed; it also recognizes invalid commands and responds with (sometimes cryptic) error messages.

DOS Path

See "Path."

DOS Prompt

The DOS prompt comprises the characters displayed on the left side of the CRT that indicate that DOS is ready for command input. The DOS prompt can be controlled by the PROMPT command to tell you all kinds of things about where and when you're working. We recommend including the command **PROMPT PG** in your AUTOEXEC.BAT file, so that DOS always displays the default directory as a part of the DOS prompt.

DOS Shell

The term "shell" originated with UNIX and is used to name the command interpreter that accepts keyboard input. In essence, the shell is a program that runs when other programs are not running and permits a user to communicate with the computer. The most common DOS shell is the DOS command interpreter (see "DOS Command Interpreter" for a definition), but it is possible to alter that interpreter or substitute a different one using the DOS SHELL command (commonly found in the CONFIG.SYS file) to make the desired changes. One of the SPCTs, ANNOY, is actually a substitute DOS shell that intercepts input that would normally go straight to the DOS command interpreter (this is, in fact, the secret of how it works).

ECHO

A DOS command that can be used to control whether or not command input is automatically written to the screen (turned on with the command ECHO ON; off with the command ECHO OFF). ECHO can also be used to write messages to the display from inside .BAT files. For example, the command **ECHO Hello World!** would cause DOS to write "Hello World!" to the CRT.

EGA (Abbreviation for *Enhanced Graphics Adapter*)

EGA was developed as a refinement of CGA by IBM, partly in response to the success of the Hercules display adapter. Its resolution was increased to 680 x 350, as was the number of pixels used for character display (resulting in sharper, more readable text displays). Likewise, the number of possible colors was increased to 64 (16 being viewable at any one time).

<Esc>

The way we denote the key labeled "Esc"on the DOS keyboard; in some DOS applications the <Esc> key is used to exit the program. In other cases, the <Esc> key is used to modify the meaning of other keys (it is used in combination with other keys). We use the angle brackets (< >) to enclose the names of specific keys so that you can easily recognize them as keys.

.EXE

A file extension for DOS executable files. Most files that end in .EXE (for example, ADULATE.EXE) are DOS applications.

Freeware

Software that is given away at no charge. By declaring a program to be freeware, the developer indicates that he or she surrenders financial interest in that program and that it can be freely copied and distributed without recompense to its creator. Several SPCTs are freeware and are indicated as such.

Gas-plasma Display

A gas-plasma display is a type of display that uses a flat panel consisting of two electrically coated glass surfaces enclosing a gas-charged vacuum. The electrical activity caused by charging a specific position on the screen (called a picture element, or pixel) excites the gas at that point, causing it to glow. Gas-plasma displays are compact (but expensive) and are popular in portable computers.

Graphics Card (a.k.a. Graphics Adapter)

A graphics card or adapter is a plug-in card that gets inserted into a PC that has been designed to drive a graphics display device. Specific types of graphics cards mentioned in this book include CGA, EGA, Hercules, and VGA.

Hercules

Hercules is the name of a company that developed an early type of PC graphics and text display card, used to drive a graphics monitor. The name Hercules has become a synonym for "Hercules-compatible," since many companies other than Hercules now make such display cards. The earliest versions supported graphics displays as well as the IBM extended character set only on monochrome displays, but later versions support color as well.

Kilobyte

A kilobyte is 2^{10}, or 1024, bytes. This is a common unit of measurement for computer memory and storage and is commonly abbreviated as K or KB.

Motherboard

A motherboard is the heart and brain of a PC: It contains the central processing unit (CPU), which for a PC is a member of Intel's 80X86 microprocessor family. It also typically includes the keyboard interface, the slots into which adapters must be inserted, and some or all of the PC's random-access memory (RAM).

Option

An option is a type of argument or parameter for a DOS command, usually one that is constrained to have a particular format or a particular value. It represents one choice among several (or many) possible choices, but it is not entirely arbitrary. In the EXPLOSIV program, the options for idle time (m$<n>$), delay (d$<n>$), and so on, represent the only possible arguments that can be used to control the program's behavior.

Parameter

A parameter is a value that is associated with a DOS command. It is a synonym for the term "argument" (see its definition for an example of a parameter/argument).

PATH

The term for the file search order established by the DOS PATH command (usually included in the AUTOEXEC.BAT file). The DOS PATH command tells DOS where to look for things if it can't find them in the current default directory (the directory where you are currently located). The PATH command can tell DOS to look in multiple directories on multiple drives, and using it is a handy way to keep all the programs and commands that you regularly use accessible no matter what your current directory may happen to be.

PKZIP

The name of a useful file compression program written by Phil Katz's PKWare company. It is a commonly used program to decrease the size of files for storage (to fit more files onto a hard or floppy disk) or for transmission (shorter files take less time to upload and download). This program is highly recommended. (See "Squeezing the Most out of the SPCT Disks" in the Introduction of this book.)

Public Domain

Software is said to be in the public domain when its developer chooses to make it freely available without restrictions on further duplication or use. From a legal standpoint, public domain means that no individual owns it, but that some individuals (or agencies) are recognized as its source. Despite the connotation, public domain software is not always free of charge, but any charges associated are supposed to be for reproduction and handling rather than as payment for its intrinsic value. Most software whose development is funded by the government is required to be placed in the public domain.

RAM (Abbreviation for *Random Access Memory*)

RAM is a form of very fast computer storage space where the CPU can read from or write to when executing programs. It provides the information needed to run programs and to supply them with data; it is also the repository for working results from a program's execution. RAM is volatile: When the computer is powered down, its contents disappear. That is why hard and floppy disks are required in PCs (and other computers), since some form of permanent storage is always needed.

Reboot

To reboot a computer is to restart it, either by entering a special key sequence (called a "soft boot" in computer jargon, because it uses software to restart itself) or by cycling the PC's power off and then back on (called a "hard boot," because it requires the use of hardware—the on/off switch).

ROM (Abbreviation for *Read-Only Memory*)

A type of computer storage in which information gets "burned into" particular circuits. It can be read as many times as needed, but it cannot be changed. ROM is usually slower than RAM, but it is sufficiently faster than disks to warrant its use for regularly used programs (the PC uses ROM for its startup routines and for its Basic Input Output System, or BIOS).

Screen Blanker

A program that monitors keyboard activity, keeping track of how long it has been idle. Screen blankers take over the computer display after a certain idle period has elapsed, creating purposely random images. If CRTs sit idle displaying the same image a large part of the time (for example, the C:\> prompt), the image can actually get burned into a computer display over time. Screen blankers prevent this kind of wear by making sure that all parts of the screen are kept equally active. For this reason, they are very popular pieces of software because most users tend to leave their computers running but idle much of the time.

Shareware

Software that may be freely distributed but whose creators normally request that regular or habitual users help to support the programmer by remitting a fee (usually very reasonable). Shareware authors generally retain the copyright to their work and prohibit others from reselling it without their permission. (Of course, we have permission to redistribute all the shareware we've included in this book.) Many of the SPCTs in this book are shareware, and we ask yet again that you send your checks or money orders for those programs that you find merit regular use.

SPCT (Abbreviation for _Stupid PC Trick_)

SPCTs are the subject of this book—we used an abbreviation to make life easier for all of us.

System Crash/System Hang

A PC is said to have "crashed" or "hung" when it no longer responds to keyboard input. This very often indicates that the executable image of the operating system has become damaged or corrupted. The most common cure is to reboot or restart the machine, very often with the "three-fingered salute" used to issue a warm restart command: <Ctrl>-<Alt>-<Del>. Sometimes the keyboard will not even respond to this key sequence, at which time a hard reset (turning the power switch off and on) is the only way to get back into action. Because of the need to manipulate hardware (the on/off switch), this type of crash or hang is sometimes called a "hard crash."

TSR (Abbreviation for _Terminate-and-Stay-Resident_)

A TSR is a kind of program that stays installed within DOS even when it's not in use, ready to be invoked at a single keystroke. TSRs are commonly used for utility programs, such as notepads, address and phone books, and other utilities that are handy to have instant access to. They are also used to drive devices, such as printers, tape drives, and scanners, to permit the PC to be used for other things while also communicating with one or more of these devices. See Appendix A, "Managing TSRs," for detailed information about this type of DOS program.

TSR Management Utilities

Programs that are designed to permit TSRs to be loaded and unloaded without requiring that a computer be rebooted. See Appendix A, "Managing TSRs," for more information.

VGA (Abbreviation for *Virtual Graphics Array*)

The VGA name is derived from a special-purpose integrated circuit used in the implementation of most VGA adapter cards. It supports the greatest number of on-screen colors (256) and the highest resolution (640x480) of the commonly used graphics adapters. We recommend VGA displays, since they are the sharpest and most colorful of the affordable PC graphics technologies currently available.

Working Directory

Denotes the current default directory as established by the AUTOEXEC.BAT command after reboot or startup or by subsequent CD commands thereafter. It is called the working directory, because that is where one is assumed to be working.

.ZIP

An extension commonly used to indicate a file that has been compressed using the PKWare PKZIP utility. Such files must be decompressed before they can be used, typically with PKWare's PKUNZIP utility program.

ZIP2EXE

The name of a program in the PKWare compression utilities that converts .ZIP files into self-extracting programs (in other words, it converts .ZIP files to .EXE files; hence the name).

Order Form

Items for Order

We can supply the following items to you if you order them using the form on the next page. Each set of disks includes the complete contents of the tricks contained in compressed form as two 360 KB 5.25" floppies with the book.

5.25" HD (1.2 MB) floppies, decompressed   total: 2

5.25" DD (360 KB) floppies, decompressed   total: 4

3.5" HD (1.44 MB) floppies, decompressed   total: 1

3.5" DD (720 KB) floppies, decompressed   total: 2

Turbo TSR Utilities, on 3.5" DD (720 KB)
or 5.25" HD (1.2 MB) only   total: 1

Orders must be pre-paid by check or money order (all fees include shipping, handling, and sales tax where applicable). The charge is $5.00 (in U.S. currency) per disk (minimum order $10.00).

Please send all orders to:

LANWRIGHTS
5810 Lookout Mountain Dr.
Austin, TX 78731-3618

Order Form

Please send me:

Qty	Item	Unit Cost	Total
_____	5.25" HD Disks	$10.00	_____
_____	5.25" DD Disks	$20.00	_____
_____	3.5" HD Disks	$10.00	_____
_____	3.5" DD Disks	$10.00	_____
_____	Turbo TSR Utilities 3.5" DD Disks	$10.00	_____
_____	Turbo TSR Utilities 5.25" DD Disks	$10.00	_____
		Grand Total	_____

Please remit the total amount by check or money order only (no cash, please). Make checks or money orders payable in U.S. currency to **LANWRIGHTS**. Orders will be processed within 7 days for money orders and within 5 days of clearing for checks. Please fill out the ship-to address below.

Ship to:

Name: _____

Company: _____

Street: _____

City, State, ZIP: _____